100

AUSSIE

THINGS

WE KNOW AND

LOVE

(IN NO PARTICULAR ORDER)

CONTENTS

Dedicated to my decidedly un-Aussie dad, Frank Banyai, and grandfather, Wilhelm Von Pfeiffer, one of the unfortunate few to have died from a snake bite. Loving thanks to Tom Carlyon, and Clementine, Beatrix and Peppa.

AUSTRALIAN ANIMALS
THAT WANT YOU TO DIE*

* and some that would just prefer to cuddle

BLUE-RINGED OCTOPUS

Australia has something of a monopoly on miniature assassins. Sure, we're not the only place that is home to deadly creatures, but they're a little easier to spot in other countries. Our American brothers and sisters, for instance, are not at great risk of accidentally treading on a grizzly bear. Australia, though? Some of our most poisonous residents are small enough to fit into an evening clutch purse, which is something to remember next time you're choosing accessories for a Tinder date.

Blue-ringed octopus

High on the list of Australia's most dainty, yet deadly, creatures sits the blue-ringed octopus. When provoked, it will use its beak – yes, *beak* – to bite its victim and inject it with a complex neurotoxin 1200 times more potent than cyanide. And there is no antidote. Unless CPR and heart massage are commenced within minutes, death is almost certain.

The blue-ringed octopus is so petite that, were you to take leave of your senses, you could easily hold one in the palm of your hand. Each critter is about 5 centimetres long in body and 10 centimetres in arms. 'How many people could a blue-ringed octopus kill with one bite?', you ask. The answer is 26, equivalent to all the members of Cabinet, and a couple of their pets.

But if this has you considering a move to New Zealand, rest assured that like much of Australia's deadliest wildlife, the blue-ringed octopus is not aggressive by nature, and only three deaths have been attributed to blue-ringed bites since 1961. Pretty amazing when you consider their preferred habitat is shallow water, under shells and in rockpools, *and* that they are excellent camouflage artists. Their distinctive iridescent blue rings only appear when provoked, so they're not quite the screamingly obvious disco-ball of the bay one would hope them to be.

If you do have the misfortune to annoy a blue-ringed octopus and find yourself with a beak sunk in your foot, take heart – with continuous CPR and heart massage, you should walk out of the hospital 24 hours later with no further problems, save a lingering fear of the itsy-bitsy, teeny-weeny octopus in a blue polka-dot bikini.

SNAKES

A cursory glance at any reputable book, blog or website devoted to snakes will give you a very clear picture of why Australia's slithering population is to be viewed through a lens of awe and fear. Our country is home to approximately 140 varieties of snake and over half of them are venomous (much like the comments section of your average online news site).

Snakes

There are many compelling reasons to fear Australian snakes. A lot of them have venom containing complex toxins that can prevent your blood from clotting, shatter your nervous system, and cause renal failure and tissue damage. A taipan's venom can kill a human in under 45 minutes. They even keep a spare set of fangs in their mouth to slide into place should the old ones pack it in mid-kill, or in case a scout for *Australia's Next Top Model* pays a surprise visit.

The most hardcore of Australia's venomous snakes is surely the tiger snake, which can climb to a height of 10 metres, or mooch around happily underwater for up to nine minutes before it needs to resurface for a snooze on its inflatable flamingo. Tiger snakes can also make love for seven hours straight. Obviously anything that can bonk for an entire working day should be approached with extreme caution.

Having said all that, a hefty dose of perspective is required when discussing Australia's lengthy list of venomous snakes. According to experts, Australian snakes have much smaller fangs than their foreign brothers and sisters and, of the 3000 snake bites that occur every year in Australia, only 450 are envenomous (a bite in which venom is actually injected). Excellent clinical care based on decades of rigorous research has helped to greatly minimise the threat posed by snakes in Australia.

By contrast, in India, about 45,000 people die from snake bites every year. In Australia, your car poses a far greater threat to your life than any snake. Hell, your Nutribullet probably poses a greater threat to your health – those blades are sharp!

Avoiding snake bites in Australia is simply a matter of employing a little common sense. Make plenty of noise when walking in the bush, never pick up or attempt to kill a snake, and familiarise yourself with the habitats and temperaments of the most common varieties. Australian snakes are overwhelmingly just a bunch of nervous dudes, slithering around hoping to bag a long-haired rat for lunch, or, in the case of the tiger snake, find a comely mate for a torturously long tantric sex session.

SPIDERS

Spiders are synonymous with Australian life. About 10,000 species of the spindly buggers live here and a distressing percentage like to hang out in the same places we do. Scarcely a day passes that Aussies don't encounter at least a couple of spiders hiding on, or in, a bicycle, scooter, pram, tree or linen cupboard. People not raised in Australia find this remarkable, and terrible. While researching this book, I sent a text message to a German friend:

Me: As a cosmopolitan European, do you find the volume of spiders in Australia quite shocking?

Her: Yes! So many, everywhere. I once had a white-tail casually walk up my arm at my mother-in-law's house. Your deadly fauna unsettles me deeply.

SPIDERS

Well, German friend, Australia actually only has two potentially lethal spiders, the redback and the (male) Sydney funnelweb, and highly effective antivenom exists for both. Their bites are also often 'blanks', meaning no venom is delivered. In fact, no one has died of a spider bite in Australia since 1979. That might not be enough to prompt you to roll around naked in a stack of firewood, but it should at least stop you imagining your own funeral at the sight of a redback or a funnelweb.

The problem humans have with spiders has little to do with their venom. Huntsman spiders, after all, aren't very venomous, but when was the last time you invited one over for wine and cheese? Researchers have tried time and time again to pinpoint why humans are so inclined to squeal at the mere suggestion of a spider. Is it an evolutionary response? A trauma response? Some scientists argue it's simply because humans are naturally suspicious of anything with more legs than us, so our fear is simply a response to an excessive numbers of legs. If koalas had eight legs, no one would be clamouring for cuddles with them at wildlife sanctuaries.

Despite their unsettling legs and omnipresence in our car doors, Australian spiders are generally model citizens. They eat cockroaches and other annoying insects and don't care a jot for humans, regarding them simply as very large rocks that prey sometimes settle on, which is why, if you live in Sydney, by the time you turn 35 a huntsman will have crawled across your face as you sleep *at least twice*. If this fact were more widely known, perhaps homes in Sydney wouldn't be so expensive. Spread the word!

IRUKANDJI AND BOX JELLYFISH

How can something that looks like a garter belt do so much damage?

Australia's two deadliest jellyfish, the box and the Irukandji, may appear no more threatening than a dandelion at first glance, but appearances are deceiving; an encounter with an Irukandji or box jellyfish is as good as a kiss from Satan.

These two, most impolite, species of jellyfish are found in the northern waters of Australia, but you're unlikely to see them starring in any Queensland Tourism campaigns thanks to their awesome capacity to ruin a day at the beach. For starters, both are extremely hard to see. The Irukandji is just 1 to 2.5 centimetres long and while the box jellyfish is considerably bigger, at around 20 centimetres

Irukandji and box jellyfish

long, both species are transparent so you're not likely to see them coming. This is a shame because in the case of the Irukandji, although it doesn't hurt much initially, that sting can bring on Irukandji Syndrome. This means high blood pressure, vomiting, sweating, severe pain in the limbs, cardiac problems and an acute sense of doom, which seems quite reasonable given the circumstances.

The box jellyfish, meanwhile, doesn't permit you the luxury of wondering if you should seek medical assistance or not – it gets straight down to the business of killing you. In the words of CSIRO jellyfish expert Dr Lisa-Ann Gershwin, when stung by a box jellyfish you can expect to feel as though you have been 'dropped in a vat of boiling oil'. The upside is that death can occur within two minutes, so you probably won't feel that way for very long.

Both species are found elsewhere in the world but, owing to our reputation as a safe space for lethal stuff, people tend to associate Irukandji and box jellyfish with Australian beaches. Much of what we know about jellyfish is also thanks to the work of Australian scientists, who have deduced that, statistically speaking, the box jellyfish is the deadlier of the two, with 63 reported deaths since 1884. The Irukandji has clocked a comparatively civilised two deaths.

If you must go in the water but would prefer not to experience the sensation of your heart locking into a contracted state, or fall prey to Irukandji Syndrome (during which people have begged their doctors to kill them to get the pain over with), the best protection against stings is a full-body lycra or neoprene suit. And if you see a cluster of what looks like crushed ice or glass at the high tide line, stay out of the water. These are salps, one of the only living organisms on the planet that likes to hang out with Irukandji jellyfish.

Having said all that, don't waste too much energy panicking about lethal jellyfish; there are way more things *outside* the water that will probably get you first!

CROCODILES

Realistically, we should probably be more worried about the sodium content in our cornflakes and our family history of angina than our country's abundance of lethal fauna. However, you *should* still be scared of crocodiles. Fear of crocs is not irrational, it's essential to your ongoing existence.

Crocodiles are not like other deadly animals in Australia, most of which would rather swallow a rat or make love to a jetty pole than hurt a human. No, the beady, reptilian eyes of a croc do not conceal the gentle soul of a wounded poet. To wit: each year at least two Northern Territory residents are claimed by saltwater crocs. Considering the Northern Territory has the highest concentration of saltwater and freshwater crocodiles in the world, is it any wonder they build their homes on stilts?

It's not all bad news, though. Freshwater crocs are not known to have caused any human deaths and, while they might bite in self-defence, it's not essential to prepare your will before swimming in their vicinity. That's not an invitation to go swim some laps with a freshwater croc, but if you need proof of their relatively placid nature compared to their saltwater cousins, look up 'freshwater croc vs olive python' on YouTube. Spoiler alert: after a casual five-hour tussle, the python wins.

This kind of humiliation would never befall a saltwater crocodile. Weighing in at 500 kilograms and measuring 4 to 5 metres in length, saltwater crocs are what's called a 'hypercarnivorous apex predator'. Let's break that down: a hypercarnivore is an animal

CROCODILES

with a diet of more than 70 per cent meat and an apex predator is an animal that sits at the top of the food chain and has no predators. Saltwater crocs are both. To put that in context, sharks are also hypercarnivorous apex predators, but crocodiles have been known to eat sharks, which makes them, um, hypercarnivorous apex-apex predators. Basically, don't mess with a saltwater croc.

While crocs are not the cuddliest inhabitants of the planet, they are one of the oldest, having been around for about 200 million years. This longevity has equipped them with a number of startling physical traits. For instance, the freshwater croc can perform a 'high walk' on land, which is a fancy way of saying *THEY CAN WALK LIKE HUMANS*. They also have night vision and can see underwater.

All crocodiles prefer their body temperature to sit between 30 and 33 degrees Celsius and will orientate their bodies to ensure they receive as much sun as possible. They can't sweat, so when they're at risk of overheating they either get in the water, or lay about with their jaws agape to allow cold air to circulate over the skin in their mouths. Actually, the more you learn about crocodiles, the more you realise how many characteristics they share with the Real Housewives of Sydney.

SHARKS

___

Sharks kill an average of three people per year in Australia. Meanwhile, chair-related falls claim 26 lives per year, but where are the helicopters and sirens signalling the presence of a potentially lethal chair in your home? Sure, sharks are a little more physically intimidating than a replica Eames, but still, why do we react with terror to sharks when only a few shark species have any interest in eating us?

    Their size could have something to do with it. Exact figures are hard to come by, but the largest great white shark ever caught is believed to have weighed 4500 kilograms. And then there's those teeth, which aren't exactly comforting when viewed up close. Fun fact: sharks constantly shed and replace their teeth, going through about 35,000 in a lifetime.

Sharks

Australian waters are teeming with sharks, with Western Australia and New South Wales particular hotspots. We also have the highest number of shark fatalities in the world. In 2010, five people were killed by sharks in Western Australia and attacks do appear to be increasing, but this is thought to be mostly due to an increase in the human, rather than shark, population.

Sharks are inevitably portrayed in film and print as the enemy, circling the shallows as they prepare to turn a fun family outing into a bloody catastrophe. On top of the bad press, sharks also have to contend with humanity's collective hangover from a few thousand years back, when humans were animal prey. Oceans are the last remaining space in which we maintain that ancient vulnerability – there are no guns or fences in the ocean.

According to researchers at Canada's Dalhousie University, an estimated 100 million sharks are killed every year across the globe, so clearly humans are inflicting a lot more pain on sharks than they are on us. If anyone needs signs on the beach warning of ruthless predators, it's sharks, not people. That's not to say you should plan hang time with a great white, bull, bronze whaler or tiger shark any time soon. They do, after all, eat baby seals.

There's not much chance you're going to meet a shark in your lifetime, though. Since records began in 1791, there have been 877 shark attacks in Australia, but a 2013 research paper by shark researchers at the Mote Marine Laboratory in the USA suggests many of these 'attacks' would be more accurately described as 'encounters', i.e. there was no physical contact or injury.

The ocean will always be dangerous, but sharks are a tiny part of that danger. Around 280 people drown in Australia every year and a further 10,000 people are rescued by surf lifesavers so it's rips, rather than fins, we should learn to look for before getting in the water.

KOALAS

How much can a koala bear? Well, for starters, it's not a bear at all. Despite its famously cuddly appearance, the koala – Australia's most famous marsupial, apart from the kangaroo – has as much in common with a bear as your grandpa does with Liberace (unless, of course, your grandpa *is* Liberace).

One of the koala's many endearing features is the way females care for their young, keeping them pouch-bound for six months before allowing them to hitch a ride on Mum's back for the first year.

AUSTRALIAN ANIMALS THAT WANT YOU TO DIE*

KOALAS

Koalas are, to put it mildly, quite fond of eucalyptus trees. In fact, they don't often leave them, sleeping up to 18 hours a day in their forks and nooks. They don't have to worry about falling out either, as their opposable digits and extremely sharp claws help them stay exactly where they want to be. In the six hours a day that they aren't competing with domestic cats to be the world's best sleepers, they feed on the eucalyptus tree's leaves, which also satisfies most of their water requirements.

Koalas love eucalyptus leaves so much, they consume a disproportionately high amount for their body size (around 1.1 kilogram) per day. For safe keeping, they store snack-sized amounts of the leaves in their cheeks and pouches. (Try doing that around the house and see if anyone thinks you're as cute as a koala.) The vast quantities they consume leave them with a distinctive scent of eucalyptus oil, similar to the stuff you use to make pillowcases smell less like drool.

Eucalyptus leaves are an odd choice of food to binge on given they have low nutritive content, are toxic and require huge amounts of energy to digest. This is why koalas sleep so much; it's not, as is commonly believed, because of any narcotic properties in the leaves. In other words, don't try to get high on eucalyptus leaves.

You may be wondering how on Earth it's possible for a relatively small animal to ingest all that toxic roughage without winding up with a gastric blockage? The answer lies in the special properties of a koala's digestive system. It has a long gut that breaks down the leaves while protecting it from being poisoned.

Koalas are loved around the globe, but that hasn't stopped their population from declining to perilously low levels. Each koala needs about 100 trees to survive and, as our forests shrink, the koala's ongoing longevity is threatened, making the question 'How much can a koala bear?' a real and grave one.

Kangaroos

'Do you ride to school on a kangaroo?' We've all been asked it and that's OK. Every nation must put up with tedious stereotypes. Australians, for instance, tend to think that Brits spend all their leisure time drinking tepid cups of tea and contemplating the rain (to be fair, there is some truth to the stereotype).

AUSTRALIAN ANIMALS THAT WANT YOU TO DIE*

KANGAROOS

Australians might not ride to school or work on kangaroos but it's not hard to see why the world wants to believe we do. The kangaroo's charms and curiosities are manifold. Female kangaroos, for example, can determine the sex of their offspring without having to subsist on a diet of spinach and yoghurt to sway the odds like female humans try to do if they want a baby girl. Female kangaroos can also delay gestation if there are poor environmental conditions that might reduce the likelihood of their young surviving.

Kangaroos are herbivores and spend the cool parts of the days foraging for plants and grass. By noon, they've had it with the sun and dig out shallow holes to nap in. They're well-equipped to cope in arid conditions and are able to regulate their body chemistry to adapt during droughts, when female kangaroos can even make themselves infertile, switching it back on when rainfall increases. The adaptability of kangaroos may explain their huge numbers; there are more roos than humans in Australia but, despite outnumbering us, they pose no real threat unless provoked. However, if you feed one at a zoo and run out of food while it's still hungry, it will scratch you on the nose.*

But perhaps the most distinguishing feature of a roo is its skeletal structure. Kangaroos are bipedal animals and can't walk. Their hind legs do not work independently of one another except when swimming, which they are rather good at, sometimes hopping into water to evade, then drown, their predators (of which there are few). Kangaroos instead hop, or bounce, doing so with remarkable speed and efficiency. The elegance of a kangaroo in motion, travelling up to 9 metres in one jump and reaching heights of up to 10 metres, is a jaw-dropping sight for us clunky humans, confined as we are to our flightless, one-foot-in-front-of-the-other shuffle through life.

*In my experience.

KELPIES

Who am I?

I am an essential part of the Australian workforce and can run up to 60 kilometres a day and do it all again the next morning. My herding instincts are the stuff of legend and some historians believe that without my help, Australia's sheep flocks would not have been able to inhabit harsh inland areas, meaning the wool industry as we know it would not exist. I have a weather-resistant outer coat and recent tests show I'm actually part dingo. I even herd reindeer in the Arctic, which is not nearly as much fun as bullying sheep, just so you know.

Yes, Virginia, I am a kelpie.

It's often said that Australia rode to economic success on the sheep's back. And on that sheep's back was the irrepressible kelpie, tirelessly herding and mustering. The contribution of a good kelpie on Australian farms is estimated at up to $40,000, which is not a bad return on investment. Kelpies are regarded as an essential element of the rural workforce, able to do the work of four humans. They also never tire of the thrill of herding. Ted, a kelpie that fetched a record $9000 at auction in 2011, was described by his new owner, a sheep stud owner, as 'the Cadel Evans of the kelpie world'.

The first kelpie was born near Casterton, Victoria, around 1872 and named 'kelpie' after the mythological shape-shifting water spirit of Celtic folklore. Rumours abound that the first kelpie was fathered by a dingo, and DNA analysis shows that there are three to four per cent dingo markers present in the kelpie strain.

KELPIES

Needless to say, kelpies aren't city dogs, unless the city in question is a post-apocalyptic landscape populated only by sheep. Unless they have room to run around like, well, dogs, kelpies will not stop until they drop. They'll also herd other dogs, pets and animals whether they like it or not. Yet another reason why the kelpie is the number-one friend of the sheep farmer and the number-one enemy of cats.

WOMBATS

How would you like to be defined by what kind of nose you have? 'Oh, there's Bunny. She's a ski-nosed *Homo sapiens*. Have you met her partner, Tom? Nice guy, for a large-nostrilled *Homo sapiens*.'

Spare a thought, then, for wombats, our fattest, beariest native animal, divided into two basic groups, the hairy-nosed and the bare-nosed or 'common' wombat. Inelegant names aside, wombats are yet another example of Australia's endlessly fascinating fauna. Do you have a hole that needs digging? Forget hiring a tradie, get yourself a wombat. They have a ceaseless drive to dig, which has often put them on an unfortunate collision course with farmers and ranchers, who despair at the

WOMBATS

damage wrought to their fields and pastures. Despite being protected everywhere but Victoria, common wombats are still often hunted as vermin, and sometimes just for sport, which seems a touch severe. Have these people never read Jackie French's adorable children's book, *Diary of a Wombat*? (In which, it must be said, the human protagonists do slightly lose their minds at the wombat's endlessly destructive ways in the yard).

Described by some as looking like a cross between a bear, a pig and a gopher, wombats have short legs, small heads, broad, short feet and long claws, which never stop growing. An adult wombat is about as big as a medium-sized dog but, unlike dogs, wombats have no interest in leftover chops, eschewing meat and eating only vegetable matter. They might be perceived as slow and somewhat sloth-like, but can sprint at 40 kilometres per hour when threatened. Like most marsupials, they have a pouch for their young but, unlike other marsupials, the wombat's faces backward, opening at the bottom rather than toward the chest. It's an ingenious evolutionary feature that prevents dirt and debris from entering the pouch as they burrow.

Another neat feature? A wombat's poo is cube-shaped and, while they might like to dig, they have no interest in burying the 80 to 100 poos they do each night. They use it to mark their territory, which they do by carefully depositing it atop fresh mushrooms, fallen trees and rocks. The cube shape helps to ensure it doesn't roll off. So, if you see something in the forest that looks like a dark brown sugar cube, it is recommended you do not pop it in your thermos of tea.

Wombats don't just use their backsides for producing unusually shaped faeces; a wombat's bum also provides a highly effective defence mechanism. When confronted by predators in their burrows, they use a large solid plate on their rear to crush an attacker to death against the roof.

So, if you go down to the woods today, don't take on a wombat in a burrow and definitely don't eat those brown cubes.

CANE TOADS

The saying 'a face only a mother could love one' may well have been inspired by the cane toad. These prodigious predators are native to South and Central America, but are now inextricably linked to Queensland, where they are famously endemic and widely loathed. How loathed? Let's just say killing cane toads – using creative methods like hairspray and a lighter, whacking them with a shovel or golf club, or simply running them over with your car – is something of a sport.

In 1935, in a well-intentioned but ultimately disastrous move, 102 of the poppets were introduced into Australia to help manage a problem with greyback and frenchi beetles, which were decimating Queensland's sugarcane crops. Evidently, the toads took a shine to the place. In a miserable irony, the cane toads could not reach the height required to eat the beetles they were supposed to control, so it turned out to be a lose-lose situation.

The effects of their introduction are well-known: cane toads are damaging to just about every species in the country and studies demonstrate that their eggs, hatchlings and tadpoles are toxic to many native aquatic predators. They store their toxin in two glands behind their ears and when administered, the toxin makes its victim's heart beat faster, all the better to speed up the delivery of the poison. They have not caused any human fatalities in Australia, but people overseas have died from eating them, and if your dog or cat licks one, you've got about 30 minutes to say your farewells.

There are no diseases or predators in Australia capable of controlling cane toad populations. Only spiders, particularly native tarantulas, have shown any form when it comes to killing them. We're talking about a toad whose toxin kills tiger snakes, red-bellied black snakes, crocodiles and kangaroos, so the take-home message here is: Don't mess with tarantulas!

CANE TOADS

Australian cane toads also travel faster and further than other cane toads in the world, travelling up to 1 kilometre per night. They are driven to keep spreading by an 'invader' gene and, chillingly, have evolved to move in straight lines, never deviating from their forward march.

If you need any incentive not to make love to a cane toad, you might be interested to learn that when the male cane toad finds a mate, he seizes her forelegs and grabs her under the armpits. If the female isn't enjoying herself, she is able to make her body vibrate to unsettle her suitor (though this hardly seems like a turn-off).

But let's finish on a positive note. It seems that cane toad venom may be a weapon in the fight against cancer. A study conducted by the University of Queensland's pharmacy school found cane toad poison may kill cancerous prostate cells, while sparing healthy cells. It also appears that native Australian animals are adapting their behaviour and physiology to help protect themselves against cane toads. Maybe, just maybe, the cane toad will become our friend, rather than our foe. Just remember not to kiss one.

AUSTRALIAN

ROYALTY

DAME EDNA EVERAGE

Just how iconic can a comedic creation become? Macmillan answered this question in 1989 when they published the autobiography of Dame Edna Everage in their nonfiction list. Try explaining *that* to aliens when they land: 'No, she's not a real person, she's a character played by a man called Barry Humphries. It's an autobiography of a character, written in character. Yes, it's pure fiction. Yes, it's in the nonfiction section. What part of this don't you understand?'

DAME EDNA EVERAGE

According to her autobiography, Edna Everage was born and raised in Wagga Wagga, New South Wales, before moving to the Melbourne suburb of Moonee Ponds and marrying Norm Everage, who died in 1988 after suffering for many years from what Edna termed a 'testicular murmur'.

In reality, Edna was born on a Melbourne stage in 1955. She is a brilliantly awful caricature of a smilingly vicious suburban housewife, and her greatest joy in life is the petty foibles and misfortunes of others. A frequent chat show guest, and sometimes host, she takes the soft approach with no one, skewering A-listers with a steady succession of perfectly vile insults delivered with her distinctive, wincingly condescending Australian accent.

It's this aptitude with an insult, combined with flagrantly bonkers costumes, that has helped her gain worldwide fame with an audience for whom many of the overtly Australian references (and there are many) mean little. It was deliciously satisfying to watch Dame Edna on the late Joan Rivers' talk show, with giant cockatoos sewn to her sequined gown, address the audience as 'possums' before sharing stories about her travel companion and bridesmaid Madge Allsop, and letting it be known that the Queen comes to stay with Edna whenever she's in Melbourne – 'She has her own shelf in the fridge'.

Clive James best summed up Edna when he described what happens to Barry Humphries when he inhabits his most famous character: 'The Devil gets into him, and he seems to welcome the invasion. Certainly, Edna welcomes the invasion. She would, being a witch.'

SHANE WARNE

Some people (me) believe Shane Warne was conceived not in the conventional way, but in a laboratory, by government scientists tasked with creating the quintessential Australian male. If this really is how Warnie happened, let me offer my most awed congratulations to those scientists. Mission accomplished.

Shane Warne

Even if you're in the quiet minority of Australians not riveted by cricket, you will likely know a lot more about Shane Warne than entirely necessary. Shane is an average Aussie bloke living an extraordinary life. His is the life your bogan cousin might live if he had the means. Said Warne of food: 'My diet is still pizzas, chips, toasted-cheese sandwiches and milkshakes. I have the occasional six-week burst where I stick to fruit and cereal. It bloody kills me.'

He provides endless grist for the gossip columns: Look! It's Warnie advertising hair-replacement services. Look! Warnie ordered a carton of baked beans while on tour in India because he doesn't like the spicy stuff. Look! Warnie got caught cavorting with strippers. Look! Warnie got caught cavorting with a nurse. Look! Warnie is cavorting with a Hollywood pin-up. He is perhaps Australia's most prolific cavorter.

It's easy to forget, among the bribery scandals, beer and boobs, that Shane Warne actually revolutionised cricket. At the time of Warne's debut, cricket was not in its most exciting period. Fast bowlers had dominated the game for nearly 20 years and the art of leg spin was thought to be dying. With his mastery of this exceptionally difficult skill, Warne ushered in a new era of cricket, influencing the game in a way that few others in Australian history have managed. He even came fourth in the Wisden Cricketers of the Century list in 2000.

Writer Gideon Haigh said on the announcement of Warne's retirement: 'It was said of Augustus that he found Rome brick and left it marble: the same is true of Warne and spin bowling.'

He may not be sophisticated, but who cares? He's one of the finest sportsmen in history and he was made right here in Australia at the CSIRO labs. Aussie Aussie Aussie, Oi Oi Oi!

PAUL KELLY

The sound of Australia could simply be described as cockatoos, kookaburras, magpies – and Paul Kelly. It's hard not to get bogged down in muddy cliché when writing about the man revered as Australia's greatest songwriter. The emotional reach of his songs has prompted so much awed analysis already.

AUSTRALIAN ROYALTY

PAUL KELLY

Kelly seems to have been born with a voice and vocabulary that perfectly capture the nuances of Australian life that we're all aware of but can scarcely begin to articulate, much less write reams of magisterial pop music about. Are you a homesick Australian in London, Berlin, or Madrid? Paul Kelly has a song to sharpen your longing a little more – about 22 studio albums worth, in fact. He probably has many more lying around his home, just waiting to soundtrack a memory you're yet to make.

Homesick at Christmas? There's a song for that:

I guess the brothers are driving down from Queensland and Stella's flying in from the coast
They say it's gonna be a hundred degrees, even more maybe, but that won't stop the roast
Who's gonna make the gravy now? I bet it won't taste the same
Just add flour, salt, a little red wine

— 'How to Make Gravy'

Missing the decayed, woozy glamour of St Kilda, or the garish charms of Kings Cross? There's a song for that, too.

From St Kilda to Kings Cross is 13 hours on a bus
I pressed my face against the glass and watched the white lines rushing past
And all around me felt like all inside me
And my body left me and my soul went running

— 'From St Kilda to Kings Cross'

You don't need to have actually taken a bus from St Kilda to Kings Cross to know *exactly* the feeling Kelly describes, which is why he is so often described as singing the stories of our lives. It's much more than recognisable place names that imprint his songs into the parts of your brain associated with love, sex, longing and family – the universal stuff.

Don Bradman

'Am I an icon?' you might sometimes ask. 'Do I hold a unique place in the hearts of Australian men, women, and children? Will my death prompt an avalanche of laudatory eulogies and a top slot in the nightly news? Will the newspapers report my death with the front-page headline: 'There's an extra star in the sky tonight'? A good way to see if you've reached icon status is to visit your birthplace and see if it's been turned into a museum. Don Bradman passes the icon test on this count – the Cootamundra home in which he was born is now the Bradman Birthplace Museum.

Bradman, widely regarded as one of the greatest sportsmen of all time, did not wear his icon status comfortably and found his immense fame and popularity 'embarrassing'. Often plagued with ill health, in part due to the adulation and expectation that accompanied his fame, Bradman remains as famous in death as he was in life.

Emerging from the regional New South Wales town of Bowral, Bradman spent his youth obsessively practicing with a cricket stump and golf ball before making a speedy

Don Bradman

ascent into the top echelons of cricket. He buoyed Australian spirits during the Great Depression, first captaining the Australian Test team from 1936 through to 1948, during which Australia never lost a series. Few players can say they literally changed the game, but Bradman did when the British Test team devised a fast bowling tactic called 'bodyline' specifically to combat Bradman's superhuman batting ability for their 1932–33 Ashes tour of Australia.

Further proof of Bradman's lofty stature is evidenced in the law passed by former Prime Minister and avowed Bradman fanatic, John Howard, which forbids corporations to suggest they have ties with Bradman should none exist. It's worth noting that this distinction puts him in the company of the British royal family and Saint Mary MacKillop, proving that you really can do anything you want when you're the prime minister. Howard also included a question about 'The Don' in the Australian citizenship test.

Even if your devotion to Bradman isn't on the level of John Howard's, there is no denying his contribution to sport. His career achievements read like a shopping list for the preternaturally gifted. He was bestowed with weighty titles like: 'Sportsman of the century'; captain of the 'greatest team of the century' (the 1948 Australian cricket team); Wisden Cricketer of the Century; not to mention the knighthood he received for services to the game following his retirement in 1948, the only Australian cricketer ever to receive such an honour.

It wasn't all victory for Bradman though. He went out on a particularly cruel note in his final Test innings; bowled for a duck. If he'd scored just four runs, he would have retired with a Test batting average of 100. Instead, the number 99.94 is now forever part of cricket folklore. Still, Bradman's 99.94 average is often held up as the single greatest achievement by an individual in any sport and, as a sign of how much Australia has taken it to heart, the Australian Broadcasting Corporation's PO box number is 9994 in honour of Bradman's achievement.

BOB HAWKE

Bob Hawke is our third longest-serving prime minister ever, a fierce intellectual who unabashedly wore his heart on his sleeve throughout his political career. Hawke achieved a stellar roll call of notable feats during his time in office, including floating the Aussie dollar and creating Medicare, Family Assistance and superannuation pension schemes for all workers. Hawke wore the contradictions within his character comfortably; on the one hand, he was the recipient of a Rhodes Scholarship to Oxford, graduating with a Bachelor of Letters in 1955 after completing his thesis on the history of wage-fixing in Australia. On the less academic end of the spectrum, he achieved a world record in drinking when he downed 1.4 litres of beer in 11 seconds. He continues, in his late 80s, to show a remarkable willingness to scull a pint for the cameras.

Bob Hawke

Australia's only South Australian–born prime minister, Hawke was born in 1929 to congregational minister Clem Hawke and his wife, a former teacher, Ellie. Before entering parliament, Hawke had a long career with the Australian Council of Trade Unions (ACTU) and was its president from 1970 to 1980. He went on to lead the Labor party and was elected prime minister; he came into office with the highest approval ratings of any prime minister in Australian history. But it was his personal life, rather than his political feats, that generated the serious column inches. Hawke left his wife, Hazel, in 1995, after falling for his biographer, the whip-smart glamour bomb Blanche D'Alpuget. Their very public displays of ardour, plus an infamous appearance in *Woman's Day* clad in terry towelling robes, didn't sit particularly well with the public, and Hawke's popularity slid in the years after his prime ministership.

Renewed appreciation for Hawke's political accomplishments, combined with a general sense of weariness about our ever-changing roster of prime ministers, has seen him enjoy a second wave of popularity in his twilight years. Maybe it's because Hawke reminds us of the days when politicians were permitted to publicly display the characteristics of a human being, rather than those of an automated public announcement device with hair.

To fully appreciate what we no longer have, you might want to ask yourself if you can imagine Malcolm Turnbull, Tony Abbott, Julia Gillard or Kevin Rudd gleefully declaring that 'any boss who sacks anyone for not turning up today is a bum', as Hawke famously did after the *Australia II* won the America's Cup in 1983. Can you?

Yeah, nah.

BOGANS

You could devote an entire book to bogans and more than one author has. The bogan needs no introduction, probably because he's your neighbour, your mechanic, or you. Every Australian, no matter their social or economic status, has a smidge of bogan in them. Admittedly, the degree varies. Michael Clarke might be a meticulously groomed millionaire but he's still a bogan – the man married a Kyly with two Ys for heaven's sake.

A bogan is not easily defined but, at a pinch, could be described as someone who has not bothered to conceal the unreconstructed aspects of their personality; someone who would rather watch six hours of *Big Brother* than one hour of *SBS World News*. A bogan is always assumed, fairly or otherwise, to be anti-intellectual and represents the side of the Aussie persona that 'nice' people try to eschew. The word originated in Melbourne in the late 1970s and is now nationally recognised.

Like flowers, there are many species of bogan, each blooming at different times of the year. Moi? I'm an ethnic bogan (or wogan, you figure it out). Let's find out where *you* reside on the bogan spectrum...

Bogans

CLASSIC BOGAN – The original and the best. The classic bogan of Australian folklore wears blue singlets, thongs, is incapable of pronouncing 'ing' at the end of words, speaks in a laconic drawl and only watches the ABC and SBS if sexy stuff is on. The female variant is a more complex beast and cannot be easily pigeonholed; she is more likely to fall under one of the other bogan subheadings. For a forensic study of the classic male bogan, see Eric Bana's *Full Frontal* comic creation, Poida.

AUTOMOTIVE BOGAN (aka 'autoboge') – Also known as 'petrol heads', automotive bogans are fond of wearing T-shirts with slogans on them, take over the Melbourne bayside suburbs in late March (Grand Prix time) and are endemic in Bathurst come October for the Bogan Olympics, aka the Bathurst 1000. If you have a picture of Peter Brock or Ayrton Senna in your garage, you're an autoboge.

CASHED-UP BOGAN (aka 'CUB')   Shane Warne.

ETHNIC BOGAN (aka 'wogan') – Usually first-generation Australian, the ethnic bogan combines the speech patterns and mannerisms of their parents' country with those of the bogan. Classic combo. If you wrap the TV remote in plastic, Mum still cooks for you even though you're five years shy of pension age and you holiday in Bali, you're a wogan.

YOGA BOGAN (aka 'yogan') – The yoga bogan is all about attaining spiritual enlightenment via the pursuit of a bangin' bod. Lives in her Lorna Jane gym wear. Blonde, always blonde.

Perhaps you didn't recognise yourself in any of the bogan species above? Not to worry; that makes you that most contemporary of bogans – the bespoke bogan.

DAG

Dag. It's the best word ever, and it belongs to us*. Take these examples, for instance:

'He's sweet, but he's a bit of a dag. He wears socks with sandals.'

'I love Dire Straits; I'm such a dag.'

'We went to see Mum's amateur theatre group's production of *Mamma Mia!* It was pretty daggy.'

'I'm not doing anything tonight. I just feel like dagging around at home in my trackie daks.'

In the golden age of vitriol in which we live, full of F-bombs, C-bombs and explosive, profane nastiness, dag is a word pleasingly devoid of malice. If someone calls you a dag,

Dag

it's not to hurt your feelings – not too much, anyway. They're really saying, 'You're a bit of an idiot, but I've still got space for you in my heart.' It's the perfect word for letting a loved one know that freeze-framing their fashion sense in that fleeting moment when oversize technicolour knitwear was fashionable, was a grave mistake.

Like the bogan, there are many species of dag, but most commonly, a dag is taken to mean someone who doesn't care to stay abreast of current trends. There's the music dag, who was so captivated on hearing 'We Are the Champions' when they were 12 that they decided their musical explorations would begin and end with Queen. There's also subspecies, like the Andre Rieu dag – that being anyone who likes Andre Rieu – and the literary dag, who likes questionably written sci-fi, romance or historical thrillers.

Dag is rarely a straight insult (unless it's 1989 in suburban Melbourne and being shouted at you by the cool girls after seeing you dance to 'Greased Lightning' and – never mind, this isn't my autobiography). It denotes a certain amount of affection towards whoever it is directed at. Try to think of another insult that conveys that level of warmth. There isn't any.

In short, it's an industrious foot soldier in the conversational trenches, toiling away humbly while bigger, flashier insults hog the limelight. It is neither cool nor clever, nor cosmopolitan (only a dag would describe something as being cosmopolitan) which paradoxically makes it a little bit cool and a little bit clever.

It's time to introduce the benign charms of 'dag' to the wider world, a world wounded and bleeding from the horror of online comment sections. Let's teach our children that *this* is the word they should be using to lovingly insult the ones they hold dear.

*And New Zealand, as usual.

PHAR LAP

There aren't many dead national heroes you can view in a museum – their loved ones tend to favour more discreet resting places. This rule doesn't apply to Australia's most famous racehorse, though. Phar Lap, the poor bugger, isn't even afforded the dignity of having his body displayed in one piece. His skeleton is on display in the Museum of New Zealand (Te Papa Tongarewa), his 6.4 kilogram heart is in the National Museum of Australia in Canberra, and his glossy, taxidermied hide is on show in Melbourne Museum.

When your carcass is such hot property that it's on display in two different states, not to mention another country, it's a pretty good indication you were rather well-liked in life. Indeed, Phar Lap was an adored racehorse during the glum days of the Great Depression, credited with buoying the spirits of a financially and spiritually depressed nation.

Phar Lap was born on 4 October, 1926 in Timaru, New Zealand (yes! Another shared national treasure whose ownership we can tussle over!) and as a foal was considered to be a bit of a dud. Widely regarded as too big and ungainly, he was bought for the low sum of £160 ($279). Phar Lap's racing performance was underwhelming at first, but under trainer Harry Telford, he gradually began to improve. In the spring of 1929 he won the Victoria Derby and AJC Derby, among a string of other impressive wins. But it was his 1930 Melbourne Cup win that forever cemented him as a national hero.

Phar Lap

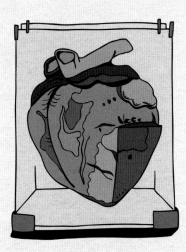

Phar Lap ran 41 races between September 1929 and March 1932 and won 36 of them. His stellar run coincided with widespread unemployment and misery in Australia, but also with the arrival of live sports coverage on the radio. Phar Lap's story was a fairytale at a time when fairytales were in short supply; the cheap, gangly horse who defied the odds to become one of the world's most famous racehorses, and his battler trainer, were passionately embraced by a nation starved of a good news story. In pubs, clubs and lounge rooms, people listened, enthralled, as Phar Lap claimed victory after victory. Blessed with astonishing stamina, he would often win a race from behind with a spectacular surge of energy in the last seconds.

But, like every fairytale, Phar Lap's had its goblins. In April 1932, at just five years of age, he was found in his stable running a high fever and in agonising pain. Speculation of poisoning ran rife, but has never been proved. Phar Lap *did* have a very high concentration of arsenic in his blood when he died, but it has never been determined if foul play was the reason for it.

Some 85 years later, Phar Lap is still a household name in Australia, perhaps the most famous – and best behaved – of all our sporting heroes.

Germaine Greer

WANTED: Role model for young women. Preferably famous for something other than her melon-esque rump, thigh gap, sex tape and/or three million Instagram devotees.

FOUND: Germaine Greer. Don't agree with everything she says? Big deal. I don't agree with all the ingredients on a packet of Tim Tams either, but this doesn't diminish my awe and affection for the iconic Australian biscuit that is ~~Germaine Greer~~ the Tim Tam.

GERMAINE GREER

It's hard to overstate ... how overused the phrase 'it's hard to overstate' is, but Germaine Greer's contribution to second-wave feminism really *can't* be overstated. The book that catapulted her to worldwide fame, *The Female Eunuch*, went on sale in October 1970 and was an immediate hit. By March the following year it had already been translated into eight languages and sold out its second print run.

Rousing, witty and grounded in good sense, *The Female Eunuch* was as steeped in joy as it was anger. Setting the tone for the rest of Greer's career, it polarised critics and readers. Women were known to wrap the book in brown paper so their husbands wouldn't see what they were reading. Greer's hope was that 'women will discover they have a will'. Women who had previously never questioned their position in society were emboldened, ending unhappy marriages and demanding their voices be heard outside the domestic sphere.

Greer's book took on previously hush-hush subjects like domestic violence, women's sexual repression, the stifling nature of the nuclear family, divorce laws, sexual harassment and the obligation to produce children. By bringing these issues into the public sphere, *The Female Eunuch* opened up debate and conversations that ultimately produced a raft of changes to existing laws and attitudes around domestic violence, divorce and reproductive rights.

Greer has continued to publish books and write on subjects as wide-ranging as menopause, Shakespeare, rage and rainforests. Her ferocious intellect and intensely charismatic, take-no-prisoners persona make her something of a lightning rod for controversy. She has been consistently accused of pot-stirring. The difference between the inflammatory rantings of a shock jock and Greer is that the latter's opinions are always infused with her tremendous knowledge of art, history, literature and biology. You may not always agree with her, but she will always make you – *force* you to – think. May she live another 80 years; we need her.

DAVID GULPILIL

David Gulpilil has played lead roles in award-winning films like *Walkabout*, *Storm Boy*, *Ten Canoes*, *The Tracker*, *Australia* and *Rabbit-Proof Fence*. He is the country's most celebrated Indigenous traditional dancer and has long mentored young traditional dancers. He's played roles in *Homicide*, *Rush* and *Boney* and hung out with John Lennon, Bob Marley, Jimi Hendrix and Marlon Brando. He's had a documentary of his life made and had a role in *Crocodile Dundee*. That's not a CV you stumble across every day.

David Gulpilil

Gulpilil's arrival on the scene signalled the end of non-Aboriginal actors playing Aboriginal characters and helped to refashion offensive and degrading representations of Aboriginal people on film and television. A Yolngu man, Gulpilil was born in 1953 in Arnhem Land. He grew up with no non-Aboriginal influences in his life and was an accomplished tracker, hunter and ceremonial dancer. His skill at the latter brought him to the attention of British filmmaker Nicholas Roeg, who was in Maningrida, where Gulpilil attended school, scouting locations for his upcoming film *Walkabout*. Roeg cast Gulpilil in the film, which drew international acclaim upon its release in 1971, and made an instant star of the 16-year-old. His skill before the camera was already taking shape before *Walkabout* made him internationally famous – the people of Arnhem Land had been performing their cultural practices for a steady stream of documentary makers since 1910.

Gulpilil has used his extraordinary grace and charisma over the long course of his career to reshape the way Aboriginal people are portrayed on screen and has incorporated his own cultural knowledge and identity into every role he played.

The burden of fame and the great sense of responsibility he feels to his people have at times made Gulpilil's life a fraught one. He has battled alcohol addiction and faced legal dramas, including stints in prison, but his commitment to making films that tell his people's stories has delivered him from the dark.

Gulpilil now lives in the Northern Territory with his people and remains a figure of great inspiration to the Aboriginal community; an example of a mainstream success who never betrayed his people or his cultural identity.

Jimmy Barnes

He was born in Scotland and still speaks in an accent flecked with the brogue of his mother country, has released four soul albums and is a practicing Buddhist, yet no other singer is as strongly associated with hard-drinking, working-class Australian men as Jimmy Barnes.

Barnes (Barnsey, to his legions of rusted-on fans) migrated to South Australia from Scotland when he was five and has had more hit albums than any other Australian artist, both in his role as front man of pub heroes Cold Chisel and as a solo performer. His distinctive raspy, soulful and – let's call a spade a spade – very loud voice is so embedded

Jimmy Barnes

in the Australian psyche that we tend to take it for granted. He's part of the landscape. It's only when you take a good look at his discography that you realise what an astonishing body of work he has under his belt: 'Khe Sahn', 'Breakfast at Sweethearts', 'Flame Trees', 'Choir Girl', 'Shipping Steel', and the song that has soundtracked millions of Australian hangovers, 'Cheap Wine'. And that's just the Chisel tunes. Top-ten solo singles include 'Too Much Ain't Enough Love', 'Lay Down Your Guns', 'When Something Is Wrong With My Baby' and, of course, 'Working Class Man', which Barnes performed at the closing ceremony of the Sydney 2000 Olympics.

Raised in the working-class suburb of Elizabeth (and just as bloody well; you wouldn't want the Working Class Man to hail from Peppermint Grove, now would you?), Barnes had a rough scrabble start to life, stained by his father's violence, alcoholism and gambling. Barnes was drinking by nine and had graduated to drugs by 11. At 17, the apprentice moulder joined Cold Chisel, the band that would take him far from the poverty and darkness of his childhood but, equally, would help to plunge him further into the abyss of addiction and madness.

Barnes became the poster-boy for boozing and pub fighting and the man himself has said the other members of Cold Chisel were, 'all decent, quiet chaps; I was just a lunatic'. At the height of his addiction, Barnes was drinking four bottles of vodka a day and taking 10 grams of cocaine and six to eight ecstasy pills, making it all the more remarkable that he not only lived (just) to tell the tale, but managed to lay down in fine detail the deprivations of his childhood and excesses of his rock 'n' roll life in his 2016 memoir, *Working Class Boy*, in the process adding 'award-winning author' to his CV.

Working Class Boy won the 'biography of the year' award at the 2017 Australian Book Industry Awards. The memoir and subsequent award, plus Barnes' work as a patron of the Choir of Hard Knocks, a choir for homeless and disadvantaged people, help to illuminate the person behind the wild-man persona – a man who may not be as 'quiet' as his Chisel bandmates, but who does a pretty good job on the 'decent' front.

Kylie Minogue

The road to icon status is paved with indignities; just ask our Kylie. Miss Minogue probably didn't imagine that one day she would be both an OBE and a Chevalier (knight) of the French government when, in 1987, she flew to England to work with bubblegum-pop maestros Stock Aitken Waterman. Despite her huge success in Australia, as a Logie award-winning actress in *Neighbours* and the singer of 1987's wildly popular 'Locomotion', Kylie's name had so little resonance with the trio that they forgot she was coming. The trio wrote 'I Should Be So Lucky' while Kylie waited outside the studio. It went on to give Kylie her first number-one UK hit. It also shot to number one in Israel, Germany, Finland, Switzerland and Hong Kong. The success of 'I Should Be So Lucky' prompted (the presumably chastened) Stock Aitken Waterman to re-record 'Locomotion' in 1988, propelling it into the top ten in 23 countries.

Born in Melbourne to Ron and Carol Minogue in 1968, Kylie was educated in the staid, leafy eastern suburbs. She started acting at age 11, landing roles in soaps *The Sullivans* and *Skyways*, before snaffling a lead in the enormously popular *The Henderson Kids*. Unceremoniously dumped after her second season on the show, Kylie then turned her attention to music, making a demo tape for *Young Talent Time*, which, for show-off children of 1980s Australia, was basically like applying to be in The Beatles. She was invited to sing on the show but, unlike sister Dannii, was not invited to be a cast member. Never mind: she had cars to fix on telly. In 1986, Kylie was cast in *Neighbours*

KYLIE MINOGUE

as the high-school dropout turned mechanic with the most Aussie name on TV, Charlene Mitchell. Her character's romance with Scott (Jason Donovan), was one of the great soap-opera romances of the decade – if not the century – and Kylie and Jason had the good sense to take the romance off-screen, devastating teenage girls and delighting magazine editors.

The romance didn't survive the rigours of life outside the comforting cocoon of the studio but, luckily for Kylie, the pop business worked out just fine. Undeterred by early critics, who felt her voice was thin and nicknamed her 'the singing budgie', Kylie went on to receive a *Guinness World Records* citation for having the most consecutive decades with top-five albums. In Australia alone, she's had eight number-one singles and four number-one albums. In 2008, she became the first woman to receive a Music Industry Trust award and, all told, she's sold 70 million records worldwide. It is highly unlikely she gives much thought to the singing budgie tag with these kind of stats under her belt.

And the brilliant thing is, even with her high-sheen visage and plummy British accent (which is probably due to the fact that she's lived most of her adult life in Britain), Kylie still has the aura of someone you wouldn't be afraid to approach in a cafe for a quick natter about life as a galaxy-busting megastar. She's a long-standing advocate for gay rights, with an enormous LGBTQI following, and has also actively promoted breast cancer awareness, since her own brush with the disease in 2005. She looks better in gold hot pants than you – that's a fact – she supports 16 different charities and she let Nick Cave pretend to kill her with a rock in the video for their duet, 'Where the Wild Roses Grow'. Budgie, schmudgie.

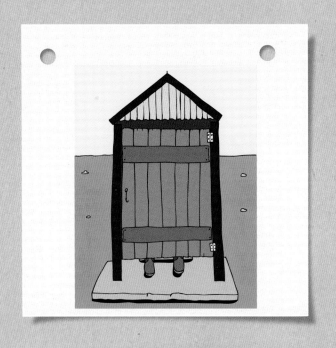

AUSTRALIAN WORDS/ SAYINGS THAT MAKE NO SENSE IN 99.999 PER CENT OF THE REST OF THE WORLD

Yeah, nah.
Nah, yeah.

You get home from work after a long day and it's time to cook dinner. Do you really want to just flop on the couch and watch *Escape to the Country*? Nah, yeah (translation: yes). Do you feel like preparing a meal of vegetables hidden in batter for your ungrateful kids? Yeah, nah (translation: no).

AUSTRALIAN WORDS/ SAYINGS THAT MAKE NO SENSE IN 99.999 PER CENT OF THE REST OF THE WORLD

Yeah, nah. Nah, yeah.

Why do we favour 'nah, yeah' or 'yeah, nah' over the conventional 'yes' or 'no'? Why is every other nation in the world capable of a straight answer except us? And why do sportspeople like saying it so much?

Got an Aussie friend who's emigrated to another country and is showing worrying signs of having lost their grasp on Aussie slang? Next time they're in town, invite them over for dinner. Give them a beer and count how many minutes it takes for them to start saying, 'yeah, nah', 'nah, yeah'. Spoiler alert: not long.

Derided by many but used by many more, 'yeah, nah' and 'nah, yeah' are not nearly as stupid as they appear at first glance. It could be argued that, far from inarticulate non-responses, they are perfectly obvious responses for a nation of people who prefer to hedge their bets. For proof of this tendency, look no further than our astonishing ability to deliver hung parliaments.

These twin phrases are also highly effective for communicating multiple reactions to a single scenario, e.g. your friend says, 'Hair shirts are sexy!' You can see her point, but you don't entirely agree with it. What do you say? 'Yeah, nah.'

It should be noted here that 'yeah, nah' and 'nah, yeah' are *not* interchangeable. They are exquisite dual phrases to have at your disposal, but their proper use is an acquired skill.

SPEWIN'

Travel is marvellous, but smoothing out all your ingrained Australian verbal tics so that people don't think you're some sort of backwater outback caricature can be tiring. Australian English is full of examples of shortened words not particularly in need of shortening, not to mention obscure rhyming slang. So, the next time you feel the veil of post-travel blues enshroud you as your plane descends through the clouds and lands on home turf after a long overseas trip, console yourself with this thought: here in Australia, alone in the world, nobody will panic and reach for a sick bucket when you tell them you're spewin' about having your five cartons of duty-free fags confiscated at customs.

AUSTRALIAN WORDS/ SAYINGS THAT MAKE NO SENSE IN 99.999 PER CENT OF THE REST OF THE WORLD

Spewin'

A true workhorse of Australian English, spewin' is the verbal equivalent of baking soda – a multi-tasking, no-frills staple that no vocabulary should be without. Why take up precious minutes of one's relatively short life coughing up sentences like 'I am not very happy about this latest turn of events' when you can simply use spewin', leaving your conversational partner in no doubt as to what your feelings are?

Let's say you're on the phone to a friend telling them about a theft at your home. The friend asks how you're coping. You *could* say, 'I am not happy about the babysitter stealing the savings I kept in a Ziploc bag in the bathroom drawer'. But that doesn't really convey the psychic trauma of such an event. On the other hand, a simple spewin' will tell your friend that you feel unhappy, ripped off, weary, and in need of a sympathetic ear. This is where spewin' really comes into its own – as a sympathetic rejoinder. Sometimes it's hard to know how to react when a friend tells you something lousy has happened. You don't want to be overly sincere and resort to platitudes, nor do you want to seem blasé. In its brute simplicity, spewin' is a beautifully Australian way of offering sincere condolences, without all the frilly, emotional (read: embarrassing) stuff.

So, next time you're struggling to find a way to express your displeasure, dispense with all notions of elegance and articulation and remember the great Aussie tradition of spewin'. Just don't use it on your doctor.

AUSTRALIAN WORDS/ SAYINGS THAT MAKE NO SENSE IN 99.999 PER CENT OF THE REST OF THE WORLD

Shortening Words

I HAD A BICKY AND A CUPPA FROM THE SERVO AND IT WAS DELISH

Selfie*. Insty. Facie. Spesh. Delish. Spenno. Chockers. Bicky. Relos. Devo. Defo. Garbo. Brickie. Postie. Servo. Prezzie. Convo.

You name it, we'll shorten it. Let me explain why.

There are only so many breaths a person gets to take in their life so it makes sense to be cautious with them. When you talk, you use a lot of breath. Talking also produces emotions, emotions raise your blood pressure and high blood pressure is bad for your health, ergo, talking kills you. Does that make sense to you? Not really? Well, hell, *you* try devising a theory that explains why Australians shorten EVERY SINGLE BLOODY WORD IN THEIR VOCABULARY.

AUSTRALIAN WORDS/ SAYINGS THAT MAKE NO SENSE IN 99.999 PER CENT OF THE REST OF THE WORLD

Shortening words

Information about how Australia came to have 4300 recorded diminutives in its lexicon is thin on the ground. 'Why use "utilise" when you could use "use"?' my journalism teacher used to say, and it's a message most Australians scarcely need reminding of. We were born to use, not utilise. No other English-speaking country has as many shortened words as we do. Australians value friendliness and informality, and abbreviating helps convey both these attributes. That's about as close to a logical explanation as you'll get.

Though shortening words has traditionally been our special talent, it seems the rest of the world is now coming around to it, primarily as a means of coping with the eight million text messages and emails we receive every day. So it's now more important than ever to let the record show that it all started here, in Australia. Here's a little intro to how we do it, guys. You're welcome.

In Australia, you don't have 'a cup of tea and a chocolate biscuit', you have a 'cuppa tea and a chocky bicky'. You do not 'meet for a barbecue in the afternoon at a friend's house in the suburbs', you are 'goin' to a barbie in the arvo at a mate's joint in the 'burbs'. You don't 'fill the car with petrol at the service station, then get some dinner at McDonald's', you 'fill 'er up at the servo and grab some din-dins at Maccas'.

In short? We are *always* in short.

*FYI, the selfie is an Australian invention. Its first known use was in 2002, by a drunk university student who injured his lip at a 21st birthday party, then, bafflingly, uploaded a photo of his busted lip to the ABC website. The caption, too long and chaotic to be reprinted, finished up with the words '... and sorry about the focus, it was a selfie.'

AUSTRALIAN WORDS/ SAYINGS THAT MAKE NO SENSE IN 99.999 PER CENT OF THE REST OF THE WORLD

TAKING THE PISS

Try saying, 'G'day, dickhead!' to a friend anywhere in the world but Australia and you likely won't have a friend much longer. Here, though, this greeting is basically shorthand for 'I love you'. Calling people you like derogatory names is just one facet of Australia's rich cultural tapestry of piss-taking. It's yet another blisteringly odd facet of everyday Australian life that foreign visitors must try to wrap their heads around. Loosely defined, taking the piss is the art of mocking someone for a particular habit or thing. For example, if your mum likes Andre Rieu, you might take the piss out of her by wildly gesticulating with an exaggerated serial-killer smile whenever a piece of classical music is playing. There are a million ways to take the piss out of someone, each one as unique as a snowflake.

Taking the piss

Taking the piss is the conversational WD40 that lubricates 99.9 per cent of light social interactions in Australia. This can appear odd to the foreign visitor, who may rightly wonder how being a bit of an a-hole can be interpreted as anything other than, well, being just that. The answer lies perhaps in our egalitarian nature. Taking the piss is a deft means of levelling the playing field, and also helps to indicate if a person is an *idiot* or a *top bloke* (FYI, women can be top blokes, too). Australians also feel shaky about overt displays of sincere admiration, so it's easier for us to say to a friend or loved one, 'I love you, drongo' (or something much worse not permitted in a G-rated book). That little 'drongo' lightens things up, tells the receiver not to get too carried away with the compliment and keeps the speaker safely within approved cultural parameters.

We may love the French and the Italians and heartily embrace their cuisine, but we haven't adopted their love of grand displays of affection, no siree. But that's OK! It would be a crushingly boring old life if we all adopted the same cultural kinks. As English social theorist Richard D Lewis writes in his book *Cross-Cultural Communication: A Visual Approach*:

> Perhaps the greatest strength of the Australian personality ... is their monumental cynicism. Australians are totally cynical of people in power or with too much wealth; they respect the little person, the 'battler', rather than the winner.

Our love of taking the piss is also, you will be pleased to learn, legally protected. In cases where a person might otherwise be infringing intellectual property rights, all is OK, as long as they are doing so for the purposes of satire and parody. This cracking little amendment to copyright laws is unique among nations. So, go ahead and take the piss. It's what the law wants you to do.

AUSTRALIAN WORDS/ SAYINGS THAT MAKE NO SENSE IN 99.999 PER CENT OF THE REST OF THE WORLD

Dunny

When a person says, 'Where's the dunnies?' are they:

a) enquiring as to where the nearest sand dunes can be found
b) trying to find their packet of Dunhill Blues
c) asking where the toilet is?

   Clearly, c) is the only sensible answer, yet this, among many others, is a uniquely Australian word that won't get you bathroom directions anywhere but within the borders of Australia. Were ordinary Australians given the opportunity to rewrite the questions of the citizenship test, it's a fair bet there'd be a lot less questions about the structure of government and a lot more about the correct Australian way to say, 'I need to go to the toilet'. We love our toilet time so much that we've elevated the humble outdoor lav, aka the dunny, into a significant cultural symbol.

   What is, and what is not, a dunny? The word used to refer only to outdoor toilets, but now encompasses indoor toilets, too. A dunny is most commonly found out the back of a house or building, but they are not dependent on the presence of another structure for their ongoing existence and can appear, apropos of nothing, in lonely stretches of outback Australia. Prior to 1965, the outdoor dunny was the only kind of dunny available to 45 per cent of Australians. Gough Whitlam, on assuming the prime ministership, insisted that all homes in cities and towns be given indoor plumbing and connection to the sewerage system. Despite the switch from the outdoor dunny to the indoor toilet, the dunny has retained its status as a significant symbol of Australian culture and history. Silverton in Western Australia, is even home to an art gallery within a dunny.

Dunny

Most Australians are able to recall an incident in their past involving an outdoor dunny, whether it be up at their Nan's place in Tweed Heads, where a lone bat resided in the dunny (OK, that's my story) or about maintaining continuous eye contact with a redback in a dunny – because we all know the best way to defend ourselves against a redback bite is *by psyching them out with our terror-stricken eyes!* (OK, that's my story, too). Other countries have outdoor toilets too, but no other country holds the dunny as dear to their collective heart as Australia. We even use it as a way of affirming one's Australian-ness – Paul

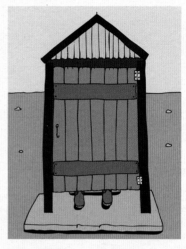

Hogan, at the height of his fame, was described as being as 'Australian as a slab off a dunny door'.

The word 'dunny' is, remarkably, derived from a French word, *dunegan*, meaning privy, but has become synonymous with Australian culture and is rarely heard in the corridors of the Loo-vre (sorry, sorry). The first printed reference appeared in the 1930s, but the dunny is believed to have been around since about the 1840s.

Since its introduction, the dunny has played unlikely muse to poets, artists and writers and has even been used by warring ex-politicians: 'Someone should take him [former federal treasurer Peter Costello] out behind the dunny and beat him up', former Liberal Party leader John Hewson said in 2009, highlighting another popular use for the outdoor dunny.

You can take the dunny out of our backyards (and thanks, Gough, we do appreciate that), but you can't take our minds out of the dunny.

AUSTRALIAN EVENTS
THAT REQUIRE
EACH CITIZEN TO
PARTICIPATE IN A
MANDATORY CELEBRATORY
BBQ OR SAUSAGE
SIZZLE

AFL and NRL Grand Final

Of all Melbourne and Sydney's diverting activities, the AFL and NRL Grand Finals, respectively, are the biggest, loudest and most unavoidable. Even people who purport to loathe football and rugby (seriously, you people need to get over yourselves and hate something useful like genocide or almond milk instead) get something out of Grand Final day, even if it's only whisper-quiet streets for the duration of the game.

As the name suggests, some pretty grand stuff happens on these days. In 2010, when St Kilda and Collingwood slogged it out in an almost unbearably tense AFL Grand Final,

AFL and NRL Grand Final

both teams finished the game on 68 points – only the third Grand Final draw in the league's history. At the rematch one week later, Collingwood snaffled the premiership by a healthy 56 points. At least no one finished the game vomiting blood and in urgent need of hospitalisation, as Dermott Brereton had during the 1989 Hawthorn vs Geelong Grand Final. Suffering two broken ribs and a ruptured kidney after being blindsided by Geelong's Mark Yeates seconds into the game, Brereton picked himself up and minutes later took a strong mark, followed by a goal; the Hawks won the premiership, and it was only post-match that doctors discovered Brereton was bleeding internally.

The NRL Grand Final, too, has seen its share of gruesome heroics: in 1970 South Sydney captain John Sattler refused to leave the field after copping a punch in the opening minutes from Manly forward John Bucknall. The punch shattered his jaw in two places, but Sattler played on, helping to propel his side to Grand Final victory.

Grand Final Day pre-match entertainment is almost as famous for its highs and lows as the game itself. The universally acknowledged lowest point in AFL Grand Final entertainment history – arguably one of the lowest points in history, full stop – came in 2011, courtesy of ageing American rocker Meat Loaf. A tuneless, bombastic 12-minute medley of horror, punctuated by shouted threats to the nonplussed crowd, saw the singer universally savaged for a bowel-clenchingly awful performance.

As Meat Loaf spectacularly demonstrated, the highlights of Grand Final day are seldom provided by the paid entertainment; they come courtesy of the excited kids kicking balls about on the street, the sense of community and atmosphere of goodwill that temporarily prevail, and the elation of the winning side and their fans. Rarely has this been more evident than in 2016, when the Western Bulldogs, a battling AFL club without the riches or glamour of some of their flashier competitors, bagged their first premiership since 1954 on a memorably feel-good Grand Final day. It's those moments of unexpected triumph that make Grand Final day one to savour.

AUSTRALIAN EVENTS THAT REQUIRE EACH CITIZEN TO PARTICIPATE IN A MANDATORY CELEBRATORY BBQ OR SAUSAGE SIZZLE

MELBOURNE CUP DAY

Earth. Early November. A UFO slows as it hovers over Flemington Racecourse. 'This looks nice, Barbara', the captain says to his wife as they land on the huge expanse of well-kept lawn conveniently encircled with protective fencing. Soon after, humans begin to arrive dressed in extraordinary garments. Women wear shoes held aloft by spikes, and curiously angled appendages on their heads. Men dress identically in pants, shirts and ties. Horses begin running around in circles while humans cling to their backs, beating them with whips. The people in hats and ties scream and jump up and down. At the end of the day, the women carry the shoes in their hands and the men lose their balance and make guttural noises. Both sexes do some vomiting.

Welcome to Melbourne Cup Day, extraterrestrial friends.

Often cited as 'the race the stops a nation', the Melbourne Cup is a 3200-metre horserace for thoroughbreds aged three years and older, and was first held in 1861. In 2000, according to the TAB, about 80 per cent of Australians placed a bet on Melbourne Cup Day. Crowd attendance is generally around 100,000 and the winner's prize money in 2016 was a whopping $3.6 million dollars, a slight improvement on the gold watch one could expect to receive on winning the Cup in 1861.

The Melbourne Cup is usually held on the first Tuesday in November, which was declared a public holiday for Victorians in 1877. On 'Cup Day', Melburnians – and some 69,000 out-of-state visitors – shrug off their conservative garb, with packed trains destined for Flemington awash with elaborate headgear, extraordinary frocks and meticulously made-up faces. Lines at the local TAB agencies extend for metres out the door.

AUSTRALIAN EVENTS THAT REQUIRE EACH CITIZEN TO PARTICIPATE IN A MANDATORY CELEBRATORY BBQ OR SAUSAGE SIZZLE

MELBOURNE CUP DAY

Memorable moments, there've been a few, and not just courtesy of the trashed patrons snaking home sans shoes. The legendary Phar Lap won the Cup in 1930 at a record 11/8 odds-on, the shortest priced favourite in the race's history. In 1996, Saintly, now considered one of the greatest horses ever to have won the Cup, delivered racing's most famous trainer, Bart Cummings, his 10th Melbourne Cup victory. It was 19 years later, in 2015, when Michelle Payne made history on the back of Prince of Penzance, becoming the first female jockey ever to take out the Cup. Her horse also beat some pretty hefty odds, being only the fourth horse in history to win at odds of 100/1.

After winning the Cup, Payne used her acceptance speech to deliver a strong message to the assembled audience about the prejudices faced by female jockeys: 'Hopefully this will help', she said. It was one of many stellar moments in the Cup's history and a reminder that beyond the glitzy marquees and champers, the racetrack abounds with stories of resilience and grit.

AUSTRALIAN EVENTS THAT REQUIRE EACH CITIZEN TO PARTICIPATE IN A MANDATORY CELEBRATORY BBQ OR SAUSAGE SIZZLE

Australia Day

Australia Day, celebrated on 26 January to commemorate the arrival in 1788 of the First Fleet, is all about acknowledging the feats of our forebears ... and eating coal-black meat. Australians celebrate all that's good and pure about our country by sending plumes of meaty smoke into the sky. It's surprising a barbecued snag hasn't been put on the Australian flag.

AUSTRALIAN EVENTS THAT REQUIRE EACH CITIZEN TO PARTICIPATE IN A MANDATORY CELEBRATORY BBQ OR SAUSAGE SIZZLE

Australia Day

Of course, our national day of pride isn't just about sinking tinnies and throwing a tray of bangers on the barbie (really, it's not). There are citizenship ceremonies, community awards, the announcement of the Australian of the Year and the Australia Day honours list. There's also an address to the nation from Her Majesty's representative in the Commonwealth, ~~Hugh Jackman~~ the Governor General, and the Triple J Hottest 100 – genuinely a big deal if you're under 30 and looking for an excuse to play a protracted drinking game.

Australia Day is ostensibly a day of national unity, but it's not a day of unity or fun for Australia's Indigenous people, given it celebrates the anniversary of the arrival of British colonists. For Aboriginal people, this day marks the beginning of a profoundly dark chapter in their history. A 2017 McNair poll found 54 per cent of Aboriginal Australians favour changing the day on which we celebrate Australia Day. However, proposals to change the date on which we celebrate have been rebuffed by a steady succession of prime ministers. So, for the time being, 26 January remains the date on which we reflect on what it is to be Australian.

Given how zealously the date is guarded, it's surprising to learn that the tradition of celebrating on 26 January is a relatively recent one. Only in 1935 did all Australian states and territories begin to use 26 January and the name Australia Day. It wasn't until 1994 that all states and territories began to mark Australia Day with a public holiday, thus permitting the entire nation to celebrate our country with another iconic Australian tradition – the bludge day.

AUSTRALIAN EVENTS THAT REQUIRE EACH CITIZEN TO PARTICIPATE IN A MANDATORY CELEBRATORY BBQ OR SAUSAGE SIZZLE

The election Day
sausage sizzle

Citizens can not be expected to decide who governs their country on an empty stomach. A breakfast smoothie of carrots, kale and cucumber won't do, either. Look me in the eye and tell me you don't feel angry and resentful after drinking veggies for brekkie. Now ask yourself: would you want a nation of angry and resentful people determining who your elected representatives are? Recent events in global political history suggest you would not. Australians have always known you can't make big decisions on an empty stomach. That's why we invented the election day sausage sizzle. America, take note: all your voting woes could have been prevented by some bangers in bread.

The election day sausage sizzle is an essential cog in the Australian democracy machine. Modest in size but not calorie content, and fulfilling your RDI of fat, sugar and salt in one tongue-scalding mouthful, the snag sates you *just* enough to feel comfortably full, but not enough to spoil your lunch, paving the way for sensible choices in the polling booth.

The first public references to the election day sausage sizzle began to appear in newspapers in 1940, and the sausage sizzle is now firmly established as a much-loved tradition. Even Snapchat has an election day sausage filter – worth noting as it's the only filter never used by a Kardashian. In 2010, sausage-locater website, Snagvotes, was launched by a group of civic-minded sausage aficionados. Intended as a forum in which

AUSTRALIAN EVENTS THAT REQUIRE EACH CITIZEN TO PARTICIPATE IN A MANDATORY CELEBRATORY BBQ OR SAUSAGE SIZZLE

THE ELECTION DAY SAUSAGE SIZZLE

to 'celebrate our democracy, encourage participation in the democratic process and offer support for community groups and volunteers that run sausage sizzles', Snagvotes features an election day sausage-sizzle map, a voting rules Snaggraphic chart and a sausage sizzle calculator and checklist.

You might think the sausage sizzle is the one and only facet of political life immune to scandal. Sadly, you'd be wrong. In 1989, then-premier of Western Australia Peter Dowding was subject to a police investigation of questionable necessity due to a 'free family sausage sizzle' he held the week before the election. Apparently, this was a potential breach of the Electoral Act, with the Labor Party accused of trying to buy votes with sausages. As political scandals go, it was hardly a sizzler. Dowding was cleared of any wrongdoing, and got his own back by accusing Liberal Party state leader Barry MacKinnon of 'being involved in the dissemination of sausages' after he was photographed during the campaign wearing a barbecue hat and apron, subsequently going down in history as the first person ever to mention the words 'sausages' and 'dissemination' in the same breath.

AUSTRALIAN EVENTS THAT REQUIRE EACH CITIZEN TO PARTICIPATE IN A MANDATORY CELEBRATORY BBQ OR SAUSAGE SIZZLE

AUSTRALIAN PLACES

New South Wales
Ocean Pools

Sharks, stingrays, jellyfish, rips, blue-ringed octopuses and eye-watering doses of chlorine. These are just some of the challenges facing Australians when they want to splash around in a body of water larger than their bath tub – unless you're from New South Wales, which is blessed with more than 100 man-made ocean pools.

For those not familiar with the concept, ocean pools are essentially the red-carpet version of ocean swimming. Carved and dug out of cliff faces to form enormous rock pools, with steps and boardwalks, the ocean pools of New South Wales are one of the state's greatest gifts to its citizens. Young, old, rich, poor, fit, fat; ocean pools are for everyone and are mostly free of charge. They offer a spectacularly scenic setting for a few laps, or for simply enjoying being tossed about by waves.

NEW SOUTH WALES OCEAN POOLS

The main purpose of ocean pools is to insulate swimmers from the deadly rips common at beaches like Bronte and North Curl Curl. They offer swimmers the chance to experience the majestic thrills of swimming in the sea, but in a relatively safe, enclosed space. Marine life does make its way in but you won't find any sharks doing laps alongside you.

The first of New South Wales' ocean pools was built in Newcastle in 1819 for Commandant James Thomas Morisset, a penal administrator who insisted on having his own private swimming pool. Unlike most of us who dream of owning a pool, he was able to order convicts to make his dream a reality. After a few months of brutal labour and cutting into the ocean rocks, the convicts had built the Commandant's Baths, later rechristened Bogey Hole after an Aboriginal word meaning 'to bathe'.

Some of New South Wales' most recognisable ocean pools are within 20 minutes of the Sydney CBD, which means those lucky Sydneysiders can knock off work at 5pm and be cooling off in an ocean pool by 5.30pm, traffic permitting (which, admittedly, it rarely does). The most famous Sydney ocean pool is the Bondi Baths, home to the legendary Bondi Icebergs. To qualify as an Iceberger, members have to meet some pretty strict requirements, including upholding a regular winter-swimming regimen for five years. Icebergers are rumoured to live forever.

About 2 kilometres south of Bondi lies the stunningly beautiful Bronte Baths, said to be the birthplace of the Australian crawl swim stroke. Further down the road, a ladies-only ocean pool can be found at McIver's Baths in Coogee. Established nearly 100 years ago, it's the perfect option for women who prefer a serene swim, sans aggressively butterflying would-be-Thorpedos.

Virtually every beach in Sydney has its own, much-loved ocean pool and there are many, many more dotted along the expansive New South Wales coast. It's hard to think of a better way to enjoy the Australian coastline, really. Now, if only someone could build me a snake-proof bushwalking trail.

GREAT BARRIER REEF

There is no shortage of things in life that fail to live up to the promise implied in their names. Miracle creams, for instance, rarely perform anything resembling a miracle ... unless you count persuading women to part with $200 for a microscopic pot of scented face glue as a miracle.

Then there are the things that *do* live up to their name. No, not the Big Pineapple, which admittedly is both big, and a pineapple. I'm talking about the Great Barrier Reef, which truly deserves the superlative in its name. They could have called it the Awesomely Amazing Wondrous Mind-blowingly Magnificent Reef and it would *still* surpass visitor expectations.

Consisting of more than 2900 individual reef systems and coral cays stretching over 2300 kilometres of the Queensland coast, the Great Barrier Reef is one of the seven natural wonders of the world. Its 344,400-square-kilometre footprint is so big it can be seen from space. Millions of different marine organisms call it home and conservationist David Attenborough calls it 'one of the greatest and most splendid treasures the world possesses'. It's also the largest living structure on Earth. For comparison, the world's second largest reef, the Belize Reef in the Caribbean, is a piddling 290 kilometres long.

Any number associated with the reef is startling: 2900 reefs, 1625 species of fish, 133 species of sharks and rays, 30 species of dolphins, 14 different sea snakes (admittedly,

Great Barrier Reef

not a figure to woo tourists with), and six of the world's seven species of marine turtle. For those more concerned with what all this contributes economically: the Great Barrier Reef injects six billion dollars per year into the Australian economy, supports 69,000 jobs and welcomes two million visitors per year.

In short, it's not something we want to lose. But the reef is in grave danger from the combined threats of climate change, coastal development, poor water quality due to land-based run-off, and illegal fishing and poaching. These human influences have resulted in a 50 per cent decline in coral cover since 1985 and some experts believe the Great Barrier Reef could be gone completely by 2050, leading to catastrophic environmental and economic consequences.

So, what can you do to help ensure the continued existence of this important World Heritage–listed natural wonder? Walking or cycling wherever possible is a good start. If everyone did this, it would reduce the use of pollutants like gas and oil, which threaten marine life. Reducing your use of pesticide and fertiliser will help, too, as these can end up in the ocean. Join a beach or reef clean-up organisation and ensure the seafood you eat is sustainably fished. Use less plastic (it winds up in the ocean, choking marine life) and, if you do visit the Great Barrier Reef, only choose tour operators who are ECO-certified and support marine conservation.

After all, who wants a future in which Queensland's biggest tourist attraction is a 16-metre roadside pineapple?

ULURU

Thomas Keneally, writing about Uluru for the *New York Times* in 1986, said:

> You can stand in Yosemite and, despite its magnitude and its splendour, know that it is all a geological wonder wrought by glaciers. But you cannot stand by Uluru without feeling it is the greatest of mythic beasts, without becoming in this desert place a brother to Ahab on the flanks of Leviathan.

The feeling of wonder Keneally describes would ring true for anyone who has ever watched Uluru glow red at sunset and wept tears of wonder. Inscribed as a World Heritage site, it is revered and renowned both for its spectacular beauty and its cultural significance.

Geologically speaking, Uluru is classified as an inselberg (an isolated hill or mountain rising abruptly from a plain). It changes appearance throughout the day – from glowing red at dawn, to orange at noon, then ochre at sunset. It is also enormous, at 9.4 kilometres in circumference and more than 340 metres high. The Uluru-Kata Tjuta National Park the rock sits in covers 1325 square kilometres of arid ecosystems close to the very centre of Australia.

Uluru

The local Yankunytjatjara and Pitjantjatjara people, collectively referred to as the Anangu people, believe Uluru is physical evidence of the feats performed by their hero ancestors during the creation period, or Dreaming. The Anangu believe they are the direct descendants of these beings and are therefore responsible for the protection and management of the land in and around Uluru. Sites around it are also deemed sacred because ancestral beings are believed to have travelled through them, performing particular actions at each site. Today, these sacred sites are used for songs, rituals and ceremonies, with restrictions on who can visit, when they can visit, and what songs and rituals they must already know in order to be granted access to these sites.

The Yankunytjatjara and Pitjantjatjara people consider *all* of Uluru to have strong spiritual significance, but make a clear distinction between the areas in and around the rock which are sacred, and those that are not. Knowing where to find the waterholes and soaks formed by their ancestral beings is vital for the survival of Aboriginal people who continue to inhabit the vast arid desert areas of Australia today.

Less sacred, more vexing, is the issue of climbing Uluru, which sits high on the list of 'stuff stupid people do on holidays'. Undeterred by the abundance of signs respectfully explaining that it is culturally inappropriate, not to mention dangerous (36 people have died doing it), visitors continue to clamber up and down one of our most treasured national icons. Unfortunately, given the recent Instagram trend of balancing on the precipice of cliffs while a friend snaps a pic, it seems unlikely that idiots on holidays will relinquish the chance to be photographed atop Uluru. Wasn't it Deepak Chopra who said, 'Beauty can only truly exist when it is mounted and climbed by cheerful idiots'?*

*No. No one has ever said this. Stop climbing the rock.

GOLD COAST

Philosophers, poets and painters have long been drawn to Queensland's charmingly bohemian seaside enclave, the Gold Coast. Jokes! The Gold Coast has traditionally been a magnet for property developers, beachcombers, and intoxicated schoolies. High-rise apartment towers, half-naked meter maids, theme parks, foam parties and beach-bum postcards – that's the Gold Coast of popular imagination.

But time marches forward and, to the detriment of nude-postcard sellers, the Gold Coast has emerged from its metallic-gold cocoon to reposition itself as a burgeoning cultural hub. It's now home to a highly successful arts festival, Bleach* Festival, and is rapidly shedding its image as a gaudy, bawdy bogan mecca.

But those wistful for ye olde Gold Coast needn't worry that Sin City is now awash with art curators and performance artists. While launching a megabucks PR campaign aimed at shifting perceptions that Gold Coast is all about spandex and six packs, a local councillor noted that 'nobody does the bikini like the Gold Coast'. Old habits die hard.

GOLD COAST

The real draw of the Gold Coast, though, has never been the tacky glitz, the theme parks or, more recently, the arts. It is the supreme beauty of the coast and nearby hinterland, which is easy to lose sight of when headlines like 'DRUNK SCHOOLIE FALLS OFF 54TH FLOOR BALCONY' generate more clicks than 'THE GOLD COAST. IT'S REALLY VERY ATTRACTIVE.'

Gold Coast residents fed up with scandalous headlines can console themselves that, while much of Australia sniffles through months of foul weather, they are blessed with 300 days of sun per year, which is useful when you have the Gondwana Rainforests, Springbrook National Park, Curtis Falls and 70 kilometres of prime surf beach on your doorstep. As upsides go, you could do a lot worse.

The Nullarbor

Australia is a nation collectively afflicted with FOMOOLNTB (Fear of Missing Out On Living Near the Beach). We are the sixth largest country in the world, yet one of the most sparsely populated, with just 3.1 people per square kilometre. A whopping 85 per cent of us live within 50 kilometres of the coast. What all this means is that Australia's expansive, desolate interior is a good place to be if crowds aren't your bag.

Our most famous desert plain is the Nullarbor, stretching between Norseman in Western Australia and Ceduna in South Australia. It's home to the Eyre Highway, which at 1675 kilometres is the longest stretch of straight road in the world. The railway line that crosses the Nullarbor is the world's longest straight railway track. And if that weren't enough 'world's biggest', the Nullarbor is also the world's largest limestone karst landscape, rising from the sea more than three million years ago.

The Nullarbor

Explorer Edward John Eyre famously described the Nullarbor as a 'hideous anomaly, a blot on the face of nature, the sort of place one gets into in bad dreams'. And that was *before* he crossed it in 1841, becoming the first white man to do so. Given his distaste for the landscape, it is puzzling that he decided to go ahead and cross it at all.

While Eyre's words carry a distinct note of hysteria, he had a point. Temperatures in the Nullarbor can reach 50 degrees Celsius during the day and plummet as low as zero at night. The Spinifex and Wangai people, who had lived quite happily in the area for thousands of years before settlers began theatrically decrying its harsh conditions, called it the Oondiri, meaning 'waterless'. Edward John Eyre could have learned a thing or two about how we perceive our country from Thomas Keneally, who said of Australia's uneasy relationship with its awesome interior, '... if we call the heart of our nation dead, we render ourselves reduced humans, cultural and geographic maggots'.

There are 60 documented archaeological sites on the Nullarbor, and drawings in the Koonalda Cave, 97 kilometres north-east of Eucla, have been dated back to the Ice Age, more than 22,000 years ago.

The mystique of the enigmatic Nullarbor has been heightened by events such as the crash of US space station Skylab into Balladonia in 1979, which prompted the US government to issue an official apology to Australia. Then there was the legend of the Nullarbor Nymph, a blonde bombshell clad in kangaroo skin who supposedly inhabited the area in the 1970s. Reporters from around the world descended in the hope of sighting the wild desert babe, but it was all a hoax. The Nullarbor Nymph turned out to be Geneice Brooker, the un-nymphly named wife of a local kangaroo shooter.

Nymph or no nymph, the Nullarbor is a place of unexpected beauty and mystery.

COOBER PEDY

The first-time visitor to Coober Pedy, 845 kilometres north of Adelaide, may wonder if their bottle of Mount Franklin has been spiked with psychedelics. An arid, lunar-like landscape provides the backdrop to a town in which all the action happens underground. Famed for its abundance of shimmering opal, Coober Pedy has been used as a set for films like *Mad Max: Beyond Thunderdome*, *The Adventures of Priscilla, Queen of the Desert*, and *Pitch Black*.

The town reveals its otherworldly strangeness in things like its grassless golf course, subterranean Serbian Orthodox church and underground 'dugout' homes. It's these underground homes that are perhaps the most fascinating and mysterious aspect of Coober Pedy. In the early days of opal mining, dugouts were just that: homes created in the holes that had been dug out by opal hunters. Nowadays, they're more commonly dug into the side of hills, replete with all the modern comforts of a regular suburban home and with the sanity-saving benefit of staying at an even 23 degrees Celsius throughout the seasons. In an area known as one of the harshest physical environments in Australia, with temperatures climbing as high as 47 degrees Celsius in summer and plummeting below zero on winter nights, the dugout homes are a perfectly ingenious response to their surroundings. More than half of Coober Pedy's population occupy these burrowed-out homes, and more than one home renovation has paid for itself via the discovery of a large chunk of opal in the knocked-out walls.

COOBER PEDY

It was opal, first discovered in the area in 1915, which caused the area to rapidly fill with European migrants seeking their fortune. Today, Coober Pedy is the largest opal mining town in the world, supplying most of the world's gem-quality opal, highly sought-after due to its ability to refract light in beautiful colours. Astonishingly, the town has not been seized by large mining companies, partly because opal extraction is extremely labour-intensive, with no special techniques for narrowing down its location. Anyone with a licence and a taste for hard yakka can attempt to strike it rich. Meanwhile, opal buyers fly into the town via its tiny airstrip, briefcases bulging with cash, and leave loaded up with gems. Less sensationally, tourists 'noodle' for opal – noodling being the practice of sifting through the discarded mounds of miners' debris in search of overlooked opal.

Visitors to the town have a large range of underground hotels to choose from, with everything from utilitarian backpackers to luxe resorts on offer. If you suffer from claustrophobia, though, posh soap and soft lighting are hardly going to allay your fears. Luckily, there are a number of above-ground options, too. These offer psychological relief for the claustrophobic, but cannot compete with the climatic comforts of the dugouts, which are easily recognised at ground level by their thin, protruding ventilation pipes, topped with mesh to keep out snakes. These pipes replaced the old-style ventilation shafts, which were phased out for the protection of drunk miners who used to fall into them on their way home from the pub. When was the last time *your* council did anything to make your boozy stumble home safer? Perhaps we'd all benefit from a little Coober Pedy ingenuity ... and a chunk of opal secreted in the lounge room wall could come in handy, too.

Sydney Harbour

TripAdvisor, like most things internet-y, is a mixed blessing. On the one hand, it can offer an instant snapshot of why you should avoid a particular hotel ('There was a cat's paw in my pillowcase'), but on the other, its reviews are written by regular people, a notoriously weird lot, resulting in some of the world's most spectacular monuments receiving one-star reviews all on account of one curmudgeon's unhappy experience with a kiosk sausage roll.

Take Sydney Harbour, for example, the largest and most picturesque natural harbour in the world, universally revered for its arresting vistas and life-affirming scenic glory. It failed to impress Matthew E. of Oxford, who took to TripAdvisor to express his disappointment. He found the 'whole Harbour a bit of a letdown', lamenting the fact that in photographs the harbour is 'photoshopped to the nines' when in reality it is nothing more than 'a large, boring bridge, and a slightly sad-looking off-white small opera house'.

But don't let Matthew E. deter you from visiting Sydney. The harbour you see in photos is not photoshopped to the nines, or any other number, and is neither sad nor boring. On the contrary, it's a supermodel of a harbour, the Miranda Kerr of waterways, and if you aren't the teensiest bit impressed by it, you may want to check your meds.

Sydney real estate is some of the most expensive in the world and Wolseley Road, in the harbour-side suburb of Point Piper, is the sixth most expensive street in the world. For those of us not blessed with million-dollar pay packets, a casual stroll through the suburbs around Sydney Harbour is an exquisitely torturous lesson in how the other half lives. Around each corner lies a view more gobsmacking than the last. Even the rats around these parts look smug; they know their lives are better than yours.

Sydney Harbour

Sydney Harbour was originally a submerged river estuary, carved from sandstone 29 million years ago. The harbour itself was created around 17,000 years ago, when the sea level rose and flooded the river. Today, it's the deepest natural harbour in the world, even inspiring its own unit of measurement, the Sydharb, which is equivalent to 500 gigalitres, or the volume of water in Sydney Harbour. Indigenous Australians have called the Sydney area home for at least 30,000 years and an estimated 591 species of fish live in its harbour waters. The harbour is dotted with numerous islands rich with both Indigenous and European history, including the UNESCO World Heritage–listed Cockatoo Island, a former convict site. Most of these islands can be easily accessed by boat or ferry.

WHAT A LET DOWN!

Sydney Harbour may not have impressed Matthew E. of Oxford, but one gets the feeling Matthew E. probably thinks the canals of Venice are a bit too watery.

Wendy Whiteley's Garden

Once described as a garden to rival Monet's, Wendy Whiteley's Secret Garden sits in the Sydney harbour-side suburb of Lavender Bay, an area Wendy's husband, renowned Australian painter Brett Whiteley, likened to 'optical ecstasy'.

Shattered after Brett's death from a drug overdose in 1992, Whiteley decided to stay put in the couple's Federation-era home and channel her energies into beautifying the disused railway yard outside her front door. Owned by NSW Railways, the yard had been abandoned after the construction of the Sydney Harbour Bridge and railway line in 1932. By 1992 it was a nightmarish tangle of lantana, rusted and torn metal sheeting, plastic bags and the rotting remains of food consumed by the drug addled and homeless people who called it home.

WENDY WHITELEY'S GARDEN

With no gardening background, Wendy began the gargantuan task of clearing the land. Her artistic eye – Brett often claimed she was more talented than he was – is evident in the meandering paths, tranquil clearings dotted with benches and shelters, and the garden's sublime framing of Sydney Harbour.

Wendy and Brett's daughter, Arkie, died of cancer in 2001, aged 37. Wendy, again mauled by grief, poured ever-greater reserves of energy into the garden. It became her salvation. 'That's the best answer to grief', Whiteley told *The Australian Women's Weekly* in 2016, 'to do something creative with your life'. Arkie's and Brett's ashes are scattered throughout the garden, along with those of Wendy's mother, father, twin sister and dog. It's not uncommon to see visitors to the garden in a state of deep contemplation; it's that kind of place.

The 'guerrilla garden' may have proved Wendy's salvation, but it is also a magnificent gesture of goodwill and generosity to the public, who are free to roam the gardens 24 hours a day, 365 days a year. Wendy never asked the government's permission to turn the dormant railway line into a garden, fearing that, if she did, the answer would be no. As it turned out, they were unfussed by her work, even helping to remove some of the larger pieces of rubbish. The garden is now cherished by locals and tourists alike and has attracted a diverse range of birdlife that was not previously found in the area.

A successful campaign in 2015 to ensure the future existence of the garden saw the NSW Government issue the North Sydney Council with a new 30-year lease on the land, plus a 30-year rollover clause. So Wendy's Secret Garden will remain a patch of unsullied, verdant beauty among the residential and commercial towers that are the antithesis of everything the garden represents.

THE BIG PINEAPPLE

Oh, how we love to mock our Big Pineapple. As a matter of fact, I've done it a few times in this book already. As the name suggests, it's very large, making it an easy target.

The Big Pineapple is one of the prized 'Big Things' that popped up around the country and became roadside destinations for roaming Australian families (hoping to tick off the Big Merino, Big Lobster and Big Banana, among others). It wasn't until sometime in the 1990s when Australians became overly conscious of how our retro relics appeared to the rest of the world. Back in 1971, though, we didn't much care if foreigners thought Australia was a cultural backwater. We *knew* it was, and a 16-metre tropical fruit with a viewing deck poking out of its spikes? Well, you can keep your Eiffel Tower.

The Big Pineapple was the brainchild of Bill and Lyn Taylor, an Australian couple whose respective CVs contained no hint that they had ambitions to open one of Australia's great kitsch icons. Bill had spent 20 years working for the United Nations in New York and Lyn was an interior designer. The couple had moved back to Australia, fallen in love with the Sunshine Coast hinterland and bought a farm where they produced nuts, spices, and other tropical fruits – alongside pineapples, obviously. Deciding people needed to know more about the area's bountiful produce, they set about building a giant pineapple. As you do.

When the Big Pineapple opened, it featured two levels of information displays dedicated to the manufacturing of tropical fruit, hand-painted dioramas of pineapple plantations and a viewing deck where visitors could take in the Taylors' farm.

THE BIG PINEAPPLE

As easy as it is to poke fun at, it's worth remembering the Big Pineapple was the world's first agritourism business, drawing one million visitors a year in its heyday. Queenslanders enthusiastically embraced their spiky new attraction, descending in droves on weekends for pineapple sundaes and wacky family photos. It even featured on Charles and Diana's itinerary during their 1983 royal tour of Australia. Photographs of Diana being ferried about the theme park in one of its 'nutmobiles' (yes, that's a nut-shaped vehicle) were later picked over as evidence of the deep unhappiness in her marriage to Charles. Looking at the pictures today, you can see that Diana was certainly not living her best life.

Diana may not have enjoyed her time in the nutmobile, but Queenslanders have a special place in their heart for the Big Pineapple. It's now heritage listed, with Queensland Zoo setting up home in the grounds and new owners determined to help ensure future generations will be able to produce their own endearingly daggy family photos at the Big Pineapple, just as their forebearers did.

PARLIAMENT HOUSE

Australian politicians are very, very precious, like the Pink Star diamond or Hawaiian monk seals. They require flying machines to take them from one town to the next and some maintain large portfolios of investment properties, you know, to keep them in touch with 'hardworking Aussie battlers'. So it's no surprise then, that these magical blossoms do their work in a building that cost $1.1 billion dollars to build in the 1980s, equivalent to almost $3 billion in today's money. But it was all worth it; the virtuoso pisstaker charged with designing Parliament House ensured Australians could, quite literally, walk all over their members of parliament – the famous sloping lawns of Parliament House are directly above the halls where our fearless leaders debate the issues of the day.

Parliament House

Parliament House, sunk peaceably into the ground, nests into the Canberra landscape rather than rising bluntly from it. This is no accident; it's a statement designed to emphasise the democratic nature of government. Architect Romaldo Giurgola said of his design: 'We felt if Australia's new Parliament House was to speak honestly about its purpose, it could not be built on top of the hill as this would symbolise government imposed upon the people.' And what better way to symbolise people power than by allowing them to trample all over their elected representatives?

Canberra itself was designed with much the same ethos and was the vision of a passionate and idealistic young American architect, Walter Burley Griffin. Griffin won a competition to design Australia's new capital city, but was hamstrung by politicians and bureaucrats less enthusiastic about his vision for a bold, fresh city harmoniously incorporated into the natural environment. He resigned from the project in 1920 with not one building up and ready. His influence, however, would prove pervasive and strongly influenced Giurgola's Parliament House almost 70 years later. The building is loaded with symbols of our national identity, from the massive mosaic in the forecourt by Indigenous artist Michael Nelson Tjakamarra, to Arthur Boyd's giant tapestry of a eucalypt forest. It houses a collection of over 5000 works by prominent Australian artists and craftspeople. Much more than simple decorative touches, these works are as important to Parliament House as its architecture.

Today, Parliament House stands as one of the nation's most prominent and familiar landmarks, attracting one million visitors per year and almost as many hyperbolic slanging matches. That's one million, not one billion, which – did I mention this already?– is how much it cost to build our politicians' workplace.

Great Ocean Road

Australia abounds with sparkly jewels and gems for the intrepid adventurer to discover. There are the ones that jump up and scream 'I'M BEWDIFUL!' (Ulu_r_u, Sydney Harbour), and then there are their less flashy cousins, the ones who don't get quite as much screen time but simply sit, stern and magnificent, waiting to knock the socks off all who encounter them.

Great Ocean Road

The National Heritage–listed Great Ocean Road is one of these quiet, jaw-dropping jewels. Winding along Victoria's western coastline, the 243-kilometre stretch is also the world's largest war memorial and was constructed by returned World War I soldiers between 1919 and 1932. Awash with dramatic seascapes and sleepy coastal villages, a drive along the Great Ocean Road stirs up many a sea-change fantasy. It's not a great place to take a learner driver for their first lesson; the road's twists, turns and distracting views make it a notoriously dangerous proposition for inexperienced drivers.

Danger aside, the Great Ocean Road is a marvel, loaded with Australian icons. Bells Beach? Check. Great Otway National Park? Check. The Twelve Apostles? Check. Of all these, it's the Twelve Apostles that are the biggest drawcard – a majestic collection of limestone monoliths rising out from the sea toward the skies. They were originally lumbered with the ungainly name of the Sow and Piglets. The name was – wisely, but not accurately, as there were only ever nine visible stacks – changed to the more magisterial Twelve Apostles. With the collapse of an apostle in 2005, there are now only eight.

The Twelve Apostles' famous rock stacks were created by the constant erosion of the cliffs that began to take place between 10 and 20 million years ago. The cliffs eroded into caves, which then eroded into arches, and finally collapsed, creating the stacks we see today. In stormy weather, they look dark and foreboding; in sunshine, they appear a brilliant yellow. Their formation may have taken place over millions of years, but it's now believed that the very processes that created the limestone stacks will also cause them to disappear – possibly within the next 100 to 200 years. The good news? They'll be replaced with a completely different set of rock formations and, with any luck, future generations will come up with a better name for them than the Sow and Piglets.

Whatever the fate of the Twelve Apostles might be, the Great Ocean Road will continue to enthral visitors with its dramatic scenery and unspoiled natural beauty.

MONA

Dear Tasmania,

We would like to offer our sincere apologies about our past behaviour. We mainlanders have been complete and utter bastards to you for years with our snooty jokes about your two-headed incestuous people, your gloomy weather, your isolation, your convict history, not to mention the shape of your map. Oh, we had some laughs! But we don't laugh much anymore. Because now you have something we don't, and no, it's not the Cadbury factory.

You've got MONA and we, er, want it. The one that's carved into a 240-million-year-old cave? That one. We want its poo installation, that waterfall that spells out words, and the wall of vaginas.

We would also like those festivals, MOFO and DARK MOFO, that take over Hobart twice a year and attract a slew of international artists and performers. Can we have it, please?

In return, we will let you come and visit anytime you want! For 25 bucks a pop. Additionally, we promise not to move to Tassie and drive up your house prices when we can no longer afford to buy so much as a door handle in our own capital cities.

Your friend,

Mainland Australia

MONA

Tasmania has buckets of sublime scenery, great food, and affordable real estate. But no one on the mainland much cared for of any of that until 2011, when millionaire mathematical genius and professional gambler David Walsh poured millions of dollars of his winnings into building a modern marvel in Hobart: the Museum of Old and New Art (MONA). Walsh describes MONA as 'a subversive adult Disneyland' and anyone who's watched rapturously as the *Cloaca Professional* – a machine that replicates the human digestive system by producing a giant, actual turd – would be inclined to agree.

MONA has almost single-handedly revived tourism in Tasmania, winning the 2012 Australian Tourism Award for best new tourism development and attracting over 1.7 million visitors in its first five years of operation. MONA is regularly described as one of the world's best modern art galleries and, with so many new visitors, it's estimated to inject about $100 million per year into the Tasmanian economy.

If you visit MONA and think, 'This is amazing. I could die of happiness right here.' The good news is – you can! According to MONA's website, 'For $75k you can enjoy all the benefits of Eternity Membership: parties, catalogues, annoying pamphlets, being sucked up to. Then, when you die, we have you cremated and put in a fancy urn in the museum. Do not miss out.'

Mainlanders are positively dying of envy.

FOOD AND DRINK YOU
WON'T FIND IN PARIS

TIM TAMS

Recent research suggests that by the year 2090, Australians will have evolved to be able to perform the Tim Tam Slam – a delicate manoeuvre in which the eater bites each corner of a Tim Tam, then uses it as a straw to suck up, or 'slam', a hot drink – as soon as they draw their first earthly breath. Humans *are* designed to adapt to their circumstances, after all, and Tim Tams have been part of Australian circumstances for over 50 years. In fact, 45 million packets of the things are opened each year and 3000 are produced each minute. For perspective, only 255 new babies enter the world each minute.

Created by Ian Norris, a director of food technology at Arnott's Biscuits, Tim Tams began their inexorable march into the hearts and stomachs of Australians in 1964. They

Tim Tams

were named after the winner of the 1958 Kentucky Derby and modelled on an English biscuit called the Penguin, which kinkily implored the consumer to, 'shut your eyes, open your mouth'. Tim Tams are now owned by American food giant Campbell's but are still largely manufactured in Australia at Arnott's Sydney, Adelaide and Brisbane bakeries. No doubt Campbell's appreciates that to manufacture Tim Tams outside Australia would make as much sense as shooting a remake of *Skippy the Bush Kangaroo* in France.

Tim Tams straddle the divide between utilitarian budget bicky and luxe special-occasion *biscuit*. Unusual for a mass-produced treat, they are all killer no filler, consisting of a layer of chocolate cream sandwiched between two malted chocolate biscuits, all coated in chocolate. They are no parochial treat, either – they are the number-one biscuit in Hong Kong, were an instant hit when launched in Israel (at a cool *eight bucks* per packet) and are beloved by none other than Taylor Swift. Indonesia even has a cheese-flavoured version, but we won't comment on that given the crimes against flavour that have been perpetuated right here at home.

We are yet to see a cheese version here, but there have been some notably revolting experiments, from Tia Maria, Kahlua, pineapple, a peanut butter flavour that contained *no actual peanuts*, and a mocktail range that included pina colada and strawberry champagne. That's a crime akin to putting the Duchess of Cambridge in vinyl hotpants and a tube top. Memo to Arnott's: rest on your laurels. However many delirious variations Arnott's chooses to unleash, Tim Tams will always have a place in Australian pantries and underwear drawers (you guys store them there too, right?).

Perhaps we'll leave the final word to Cate Blanchett, who best summed up Australia's feelings about our favourite biscuit in a 1994 TV commercial in which she was granted a wish by a genie. The budding thespian requested 'a packet of Tim Tams that never runs out'. Wise choice, our Cate.

VEGEMITE

If you've recently had a baby with someone of non-Australian lineage, you might reasonably wonder which end of the gene pool it splashed around in. Will it embrace paprika, durian fruit, Century eggs, or renounce cheese kransky? Good news! You don't need to wait until your child can articulate his or her feelings about our weird Aussie ways. Try this instead:

Step 1: Place your baby in a high chair at designated meal time of choice, ideally the first feed of the day for maximum impact.

Step 2: Spread toast or bread with a thin layer of margarine, followed by a reasonable amount of Vegemite.

Step 3: Monitor your baby for signs of excitement, joy, misery, enthusiasm, disgust or gastro-esophageal reflux. A positive reaction indicates the Australian gene is strong. A negative or neutral reaction, and you should start stocking up on mortadella.

In 2014, a study found that more than 7.5 million Australians eat Vegemite every week. About 6.4 million of those people were born in Australia. This news will come as no surprise to anyone raised by immigrants, who are understandably perplexed by Australians' devotion to a concentrated yeast extract with notes of bat piss and vinegar.

The darkly seductive qualities of Vegemite can be explained, in part, by its rich umami taste. Umami is a type of amino acid that naturally occurs in many meat, fish, vegetable and dairy products. It's often called 'the fifth taste' (the other four are salty, sweet, sour and bitter). Simply put, umami means 'pleasantly savoury', and it's what compels people to eat weird stuff like Vegemite.

VEGEMITE

It's hard to overstate how much comfort can be found in a jar of Vegemite. It's the go-to food for queasy pregnant women, the mortally hungover, recovering gastro victims and in sandwiches. But our passion for Vegemite was something of a slow-burning affair. Australians hankering for a spreadable yeast extract were already taken care of courtesy of the UK's (disgusting) Marmite. It wasn't until World War II, when Vegemite supplies began to dwindle after the armed forces bought it in bulk to nourish soldiers on the battlefield, that we began to appreciate how much we really liked the stuff. By the 1950s and '60s, it was a staple in most Australian homes.

The famous 'Happy Little Vegemites' jingle and accompanying ad, depicting rosy-cheeked children fortified by vitamin B12 and salt, ran from 1954 to the 1980s and, in the rather breathless words of the manufacturer, 'has become Australia's second, unofficial anthem'. The jingle was brought out again in 2010 'to remind Australians of their love for the iconic brand'. With 22 million jars sold each year, we hardly need reminding. Vegemite will always be an easy sell in Australia – it's the rest of the world that needs convincing.

MEAT PIES

'By 1990, no Australian servo will be without an amply stocked pie oven', former prime minister Bob Hawke once said (OK, I'm paraphrasing). Thanks to the 50,000 meat pies turned out every hour by Four'N Twenty, Australia's most famous pie manufacturer, that dream is now a reality. That's a stunningly large figure, and testament to our abiding love affair with this indelicate delicacy.

The meat pie is perhaps our only non-human national icon legally permitted to contain *snouts, tendons* and *tongue roots*. And no, I cannot tell you what a tongue root is. Though the pie was most likely invented by the Egyptians, it was Australia that became the meat pie's wet nurse, metaphorically speaking, nurturing it into adulthood and gently raising its status to that of national treasure. Somewhere along the way, meat pies and football became inextricably linked, like cigarettes and cancer, with around 300,000 meat pies sold at the Melbourne Cricket Ground alone during the AFL season. It's a fair bet the ancient Egyptians did not eat their meat pies in the pelting rain while watching a bunch of men run around a field with a ball.

If you're looking for an authentic and affordable Australian experience, eating a meat pie is cheaper than climbing the Sydney Harbour Bridge – you'll probably get a bit of bonus fat around your midsection, too. In fact, the average meat pie is so loaded with fat that former New South Wales premier Bob Carr once said feeding meat pies to kids was child abuse, a statement likely inspired by a study which found the average meat pie contains between 15 and 35 grams of fat.

Meat pies

Regardless, the average Australian still eats 12 meat pies a year. If this statistic is accurate, it suggests most of us set aside one special 'meat pie day' a month, likely when we're alone in a parked car and can scream freely when stray bits of molten-hot gristle burn our crotches. There are no statistics available concerning how many tongues have been burnt by impatient pie eaters, but let's assume the number would be close to the total population of Australia. The inventor of a 30-second pocket pie-cooling device would be a very popular person. Can someone get the CSIRO onto that one, please?

Big M

In 1978, the makers of Big M correctly guessed that Australians were bored with milk-flavoured milk and secretly hankered for chocolate, strawberry and banana varieties. The product was an instant hit, in part because of an advertising campaign featuring bikini-clad women splashed with milk.

Remarkably, Big M was all the work of a government department. The newly appointed members of the Victorian Dairy Industry Authority, which had recently replaced the old Victorian Milk Board, came up with the idea of making and marketing a brand-new milk drink. It is quite extraordinary to think that a hugely successful consumer product was the work of a government department, rather than a global food giant.

Big M

Australians took to Big M as if a cow that produced chocolate-flavoured milk was all we'd ever wished for. Everyone had a favourite flavour. Mine was strawberry, but you probably had a different favourite. Maybe you were one of those freaks who liked 'egg flip'? Evidently, there were a lot of you, as it's still on sale today. (FYI, it contains a surprisingly small amount of egg, i.e. none.) I've always hated milk, yet I still get misty-eyed at the memory of my lunch-order Big M. Each sip was like a little reward for having choked down your blackening banana at play lunch. Is it possible they put a *teensy* bit of something in there to keep us coming back for more?

Sadly, the ingredients list of a strawberry Big M doesn't reveal anything suspicious. The most threatening ingredient is cochineal, a red food dye that, despite being made from crushed insects, is no threat to your health. Nutritionists seem to agree that a small carton of Big M is a wiser choice than a can of soft drink due to its relatively lower sugar content, but that endorsement hasn't been enough to prevent a steady decline in sales of flavoured milk.

While its sales may be declining, those who love Big M *really* love Big M. In 2014, the brand learnt just how seriously drinkers take their favourite flavour when it launched a new version of its classic chocolate variety with quadruple the cocoa. Consumers weren't happy, judging by the amount of vitriol that immediately appeared on the brand's social media pages. Carped one poor chap: 'Two days ago, if someone had given me the choice of only drinking one drink for the rest of my life, I would've said chocolate Big M. This morning I gave away my Big M out of disgust.' Big M took note and put the original formula back on the shelf, alongside its beefier counterpart, the Bigger Chocolate, learning in the process one of life's more meaningful lessons: do not mess with people's chocky milk.

Wizz Fizz and Fags

It's not easy finding a shopkeeper who'll sell you ciggies when you're nine. Keen to right this wrong, in 1943 Australian confectionery company Riviera launched FAGS, apparently reasoning that the next best thing to smoking a cigarette is eating a cigarette. A stick of white candy replete with realistic burning red end, FAGS permitted children and infants to work on their smoking technique well before reaching the legal age required to buy a pack of Winnie Blues.

WIZZ FIZZ AND FAGS

FAGS were renamed FADS during the 1990s because of concerns they might be promoting smoking in children – perhaps because they PROMOTED SMOKING IN CHILDREN. It also didn't help that the name had started gathering homophobic connotations. With their thrilling red tip lopped off, they rapidly lost their naughty appeal, and now, sadly, our children will never experience the simple pleasure of pretending to smoke a cigarette, then eating it.

Which brings us to Wizz Fizz. It's interesting to consider how the idea to sell a baggie of white powder to children might have been conceived. The confectioner Fyna Foods launched Wizz Fizz sherbet powder in 1966. It was pure magic for children and the stuff of nightmares for parents – lovely, white sugar without all the yucky food bits. There is *nothing* nutritionally redeeming in a packet of Wizz Fizz, and putting Disney characters on the packaging only added to its kiddie appeal. In the noughties, Disney characters were replaced with new characters like Weird Wally, Nerdy Neil and Screaming Sally (probably screaming because she'd just copped a nostril full of sherbet). Today, the packaging characters have changed again, to starkly depict the effects of a sugar high on children – deformed goblins and psychotic, red-eyed killer clowns.

Over 16 million sachets of Wizz Fizz are currently produced each year, proving that the 'I Quit Sugar' phenomenon will likely never resonate with the youngest members of the nation.

Golden Gaytime

There's nothing dark and mysterious about the Golden Gaytime. It is unambiguously delightful and satisfies every textural and taste requirement one could possibly hope for in an ice cream. The Gaytime makes every other ice cream in the freezer department look like Vlad the Impaler. It's the labrador of lickable treats, the golden retriever of gastronomy, wagging its tail and chilling out, literally. 'I will make you happy!' says the Golden Gaytime. 'I'll even let you guffaw at my funny name.'

Golden Gaytime

Streets began manufacturing the Gaytime in 1959, stoically sticking with the name even when it began to develop, in the poker-faced vernacular of Wikipedia, 'homosexual connotations'. These days, the opportunity for campy high jinx has not escaped Streets execs, who brand the packaging with slogans like 'It's hard to have a Gaytime on your own' and 'Four delicious chances to have a Gaytime'. They took it a step further in 2016, erecting (ahem) a billboard on top of Sydney's Bridge Hotel featuring another Streets icon, Bubble O'Bill, suggesting 'Gaytime?' to a Golden Gaytime, which responds with 'Whoa there, cowboy!'.

In a powerful statement of our ongoing love affair with the Gaytime, or perhaps just because the name was so excellent they couldn't help themselves, in 2016 Streets launched the Golden Gaynetto, a variation on the equally beloved Cornetto, and in early 2017 opened Gaytime 'crumb sheds' in Melbourne and Sydney. These pop-up stores invited consumers to dip their Gaytime sticks (tee hee) into one of five ridiculous crumb combinations, the most notably bonkers being a 'unicorn breath' combo, topped with vanilla crumbs, musk sticks, strawberry hard candy and edible glitter. Regrettably, it didn't come with a loaded syringe of insulin to revive the ~~victim~~ consumer.

Sadly, our dear friends and mortal enemies across the pond are deprived of the cheeky innuendo we enjoy in Australia. In New Zealand, the Golden Gaytime is known simply as the Cookie Crumble. Try getting a bunch of 12-year-olds (or 25-year-olds, or 40-year-olds) to giggle themselves stupid over the words 'Cookie Crumble'.

For services to cheap gags and deliciousness, Gaytime, we salute you!

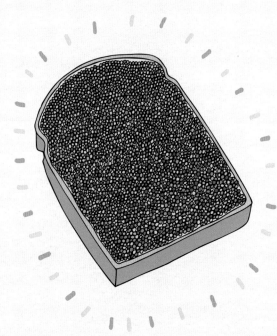

Fairy bread

To the three universal certainties in life – birth, death, and taxes – Australians can add a fourth: fairy bread at children's birthday parties. Like death, fairy bread transcends fashion, food trends, socio-economic status and good taste. It's Australia's national party food and no kid's birthday party can claim to be such a thing without at least one heaving tray of the good stuff on the table.

FOOD AND DRINK YOU WON'T FIND IN PARIS

Fairy bread

It's best not to think too much about what fairy bread actually is, though; examined under a forensic lens and stripped of pleasant childhood associations, it's a horror show. But allow me to break it down for you anyway – white bread, crudely stripped of all life-sustaining nutrients and reduced to something with the consistency of a diseased lung, liberally coated with an artery-hardening spread of Chernobyl-yellow margarine and sprinkled with garishly coloured pellets of glucose. If fairy bread were a person, it would be a serial killer disguised as a clown.

But fairy bread, as we all know, is more than the sum of its squishy parts. Your parents and grandparents had it at their birthday parties, you had it at yours and your children will have it at theirs. It is a valuable link between generations that, more often than not, are utterly befuddled by one another's habits – you're perplexed and saddened that your 12-year-old chooses selfies and Snapchat over climbing trees, and your 12-year-old thinks you're boring and stupid. But fairy bread doesn't care about any of this; it just wants everyone to be happy.

Most importantly, fairy bread is cheap. You can assemble alpine ranges of the stuff and it will still cost less than a single organic blueberry, which no kid would touch, anyway. In this age of bespoke children's birthday parties and salad cakes (look it up), it's comforting to know that no six-tier Swarovski-encrusted cream cake can compete with a simple plate of bread with sprinkles.

Centuries from now, when new life forms begin to inhabit our burned-up planet, they will find a barren, stripped earth, save for a lone piece of dried up fairy bread smushed into the ground. This discovery will provide the foundation on which a future civilisation will be built.

Cask wine

Anyone who's ever glugged cheap wine will be au fait with the demonic lure of goon, or 'cask wine' as it's known in less sophisticated nations. Ever chortled to your friends, 'Goon! It's *got* to be an Aussie invention.' Well, you're right! The idea of a giant plastic bladder (aka 'goon sack') loaded with grog was, unsurprisingly, the brainchild of an Australian man.

Thomas Angove, a winemaker from South Australia, was inspired to create the cask after learning that old goat skins were used to store wine in biblical times. He had been searching for a way to cheaply sell larger volumes of wine to his customers without compromising its shelf life (bottled wine generally spoils 3–5 days after opening). His invention – an airtight plastic bag inside a cardboard box – extended the lifespan of opened wine to around one month. He patented his invention in 1965.

Prior to the cask, Australians weren't serious wine drinkers, favouring cold beer over claret. In 1973, the average boozer consumed around 10 litres of wine per year – most people now drink that much after a rough day at the office – but by 1983, consumption had almost doubled to 19.8 litres per person, per year, thanks largely to our enthusiastic response to cheap cask wine.

Goon (derived from the word 'flagon') had, and still has, many selling points. Thanks to our complex approach to taxing booze, cask wine attracts much less tax than beer or spirits, making it famously budget friendly. It lasts longer thanks to a system called 'airless flow', which means no air enters while the wine is being poured, preventing oxidisation and is also more environmentally friendly.

Cask wine

In recent times, cask-wine producers have tried to shake off the image of goon being the drink of choice for the boozer on a budget by producing a slew of higher quality offerings. They also wave around research showing middle-aged professionals, rather than the wild teens and bedraggled old men of popular imagining, are the main consumers of cask wine. But they have quite a task ahead of them. This is, after all, the drink that inspired a dainty game called Goon of Fortune, whereby bladders of goon are pegged to a Hills Hoist, the clothesline is spun around and the person standing under the goon sack when it stops is forced to drink an agreed, and generally large, amount of wine. Has there ever been a game more Australian than that?

Victoria Bitter

A hard earned thirst needs a big cold beer, and the best cold beer is Vic.
You can get it on a plank, or doing business with a bank.
You can get it ridin', you can get it slidin'.
You can get it in a hole, or up a pole.
You can get it rollin', you can get it bowlin'.
You can get it sellin' a cow.
As a matter of fact, I've got it now.

You can also probably get it in your Uncle Baz's bar fridge.

Victoria Bitter

VB, Vitamin B, or 'Victoria Bitter' as it's known by people who are up themselves, was developed in 1854 but didn't begin to cement its reputation as the working-class beer of choice until an ad campaign in the 1960s drove home the point. Featuring true-blue Aussies at work and play over the theme from the film *The Magnificent Seven*, the ad delivered an unambiguous message: this beer is for blokes. The ads ran until 2009 when VB owner Fosters rejigged the marketing strategy in an attempt to attract a broader demographic. For the first time, the slogan was changed from 'For a hard earned thirst, you need a big cold beer, and the best cold beer is Vic, Victoria Bitter' to 'VB – The Drinking Beer'. It seems that Australians were already aware VB was a drinking beer, as in 2012 the old slogan was resurrected.

It turned out that you can lead a slick inner-urban demographic to the pub, but you can't make them drink VB. The difficulty in adjusting people's perceptions of VB was partially due to the fact it had done such an effective job of positioning itself as a symbol of old-school Aussie masculinity. This success came about not just because of the famed TV commercials. The brand invested heavily in rugby and cricket sponsorships and even released promotional David Boone and Shane Warne figurines, in the process inextricably linking themselves to a particular kind of sports-loving, blue-collar Aussie bloke.

According to the Victoria Bitter website, VB was the idea of Victoria Brewery founder and head brewer Thomas Aitken, who was 'dismayed by the quality of beers on offer in Australia back in 1854 ... and decided there ought to be a beer specially brewed for our harsh Aussie climate'. It took off almost immediately and has long been Australia's highest selling beer, despite the crowd of boutique brews and imports now vying to be our most sunk brand of grog.

If there is a man in your circle of family and friends who prides himself on being an Aussie bloke, you can confidently assume a few things about him: he will never go on a vegan diet, he doesn't drive a zippy hatchback, and he drinks VB. Nothing else.

Chiko Roll

Sometimes, a loving tribute can inadvertently become lost in translation. If you're a spring roll, you'll know *exactly* what I'm talking about. To even be mentioned in the same breath as it's franken-food imitator, the Chiko Roll, is like talking to a car-crash victim about how far over the speed limit you can get your old Torana. So, let this be an apology from Australia to China: we are sorry. We are sorry that we took your dainty snack and turned it into a deep-fried heart attack waiting to happen.

The Chiko Roll is the kind of snack you'll find in most Aussie servos or milk bars. Cabbage and the murky grey entrails of ... some animal ... are encased in impenetrable layers of tubed pastry before it's all deep-fried, frozen, deep-fried again and thrown in a paper bag.

But who cares? Well clearly, many Australians don't. The Chiko Roll has become an iconic Australian food, which is fitting for a snack originally devised to be eaten at a footy game. This is what Chiko Roll inventor Frank McEnroe had in mind when he first came up with the concept. He envisaged a sturdier version of the spring roll that could be held in one hand, perhaps taking the 'sturdy' business a bit too far (that concrete pastry!). It was originally named the Chicken Roll, a baffling choice for a product that at no point has ever contained chicken (for the record, the mysterious gluey grey meat in a Chiko Roll is mutton, which for those fortunate enough never to have experienced dinner in Australia circa 1954, is the flesh of a geriatric sheep). At the peak of its popularity in the 1970s, Australians ate 40 million Chiko Rolls per year and exported a further million to the Japanese, who to this day this are unable to explain why.

Chiko Roll

The Chiko Roll's popularity might have had something to do with its advertising. Wisely deducing that girls wearing bugger all are good at selling stuff, some ad men came up with the 'Chiko chick'. Wildly un-PC by today's standards, the Chiko chick was generally perched atop a motorbike, suggestively clutching a big wad of, um, floury dough and cabbage. Vintage Chiko chick posters now fetch large sums of money from dedicated collectors, proving that today's fish and chip shop decor could be tomorrow's ticket to Daydream Island.

The Chiko Roll's strong association with Australian youth and beach culture of the 1970s and '80s has helped it retain its iconic status even though we now eat about half the number we did then. We might be one of the world's top gastronomic destinations these days, but we still love a bit of a splash about in the deep fryer.

SURPRISING AUSTRALIAN INVENTIONS

WI-FI

Every time you upload a photo of your lunch to Instagram over your home wi-fi connection, you are benefiting from the work of Australian boffins. That's right, the technology that allows you to access high-speed internet was made possible thanks to the work of a group of Australians from the CSIRO. The wireless local area network (LAN) they invented has been fundamental in achieving quick wireless data transmission and still underpins most of the wireless communication we are so dependent on today.

Wi-fi is an alternative to the network cables used to connect devices of a LAN. Before wi-fi, the only way of connecting devices together was by running physical cables between them. Wi-fi removed the need for those cables.

WI-FI

There are now more wireless devices in the world than there are humans. It's strange to think that the careers of the Kardashian family are largely due to the work of a bunch of Australian scientists experimenting with Fourier transform calculations (and to explain what those are, one needs to have progressed beyond year 9 maths, which I have not).

In the early 1990s, Dr John O'Sullivan, an electrical engineer at the CSIRO, and his team – Diet Ostry, Graham Daniels, John Deane and Terry Percival – devised a method of efficiently transmitting and receiving an indoor wireless data signal. Prior to this, wireless data communication was hampered by the echoes and interference caused by radio signals bouncing off hard signals indoors. The CSIRO team's solution, named the 'wireless LAN', was granted a patent in the US in January 1996.

The wi-fi patent netted a respectable $500 million in licensing fees and payments for the CSIRO, but it also meant that, until the expiry of the CSIRO patent in 2013, Australian scientists frequently found themselves locked in patent infringement battles with pretty much every large PC and wireless device manufacturer in the world. To their credit, the CSIRO stood their ground and have triumphed against some of the biggest PC and wireless device manufacturers around the world.

The moral of the story is that the CSIRO should be regarded as a national jewel, deserving every cent, and then some, of its government funding. Prior to wi-fi, keeping in touch with people while travelling was a tiresome affair that meant searching fruitlessly for internet cafes, finally finding one, and then realising there were no spare computers and the room smelled like old socks; or sparring with your brother over who got to use the computer with the internet connection that night (and you *really* didn't want to use it after your brother because you'd seen his browsing history); and the agonising wait for emails from loved ones who were far from internet connectivity. Those were dark days, friends. Even darker than the ones that allow us to read *OK!* magazine on our phones under the doona at 3am.

AEROGARD

Aerogard may not have had the same seismic effect on the very nature of human existence as wi-fi, but as any mosquito can tell you, it certainly stuffed things up for insects. And, like wi-fi, it owes its existence to the CSIRO. Australian flies have a long and rich history of driving the hardiest of characters to despair, their bothersome presence inspiring the invention of the cork hat worn by swagmen, those transient folk heroes of 19th-century Australia.

Cork hats were an imperfect solution and entirely unsuitable for HRH Queen Elizabeth II. Entomologist Doug Waterhouse had been working on a fly-repellent formula when he got wind of the Queen's second official visit to Australia in 1963, so he delivered a sample of his fledgling fly repellent to her aides at Government House. The Queen was liberally sprayed with Waterhouse's chemical repellent made from N, N-diethyl-meta-toluamide, or DEET, before a game of golf. Unlike everyone else, the Queen and her entourage were untroubled by flies. Word of the chemical concoction quickly spread and pretty soon Waterhouse found himself on the receiving end of a telephone call from a Mortein employee. 'How do you make that stuff?' the affable chap enquired. Following standard CSIRO procedure at the time, Waterhouse freely disclosed the formula.

Doubtless to the ongoing chagrin of Waterhouse's family, Mortein made a motza with their miracle new insect repellent, Aerogard. It may have smelled like the inside of a chemical weapons factory, but at least it kept flies and mosquitoes at bay. Australians gratefully took to it with unbridled enthusiasm, but how exactly DEET works remains a source of ongoing debate. Until recently, the prevailing wisdom was that it confused

Aerogard

insects by dulling their sense of smell, but newer research demonstrates that its effectiveness may simply be because they hate the smell of the stuff even more than we do.

Waterhouse was still busy with inventions until his death in December 2000 at 84, and though he may not have enjoyed the financial spoils of his invention, with any luck he enjoyed the satisfaction of knowing that he helped many generations of Australians to 'avagoodweekend'.

Polymer
banknote

In 1966, a spate of counterfeiting prompted the Reserve Bank of Australia to commission the CSIRO to create a secure banknote. Earlier that year, Australia had converted from the Imperial system to a decimal currency, issuing state-of-the-art security banknotes that, the Reserve Bank believed, would help combat forgeries. Unfortunately, it took less than a year for counterfeit $10 notes to start circulating. Once word reached the public, the $10 note became an object of suspicion. The Reserve Bank issued a list of tips on how to spot the forged notes, but people were reluctant to hand them in, knowing that genuine notes would not be issued in return. Unrest around the forgeries ran so deep that at one stage, members of the Engineering Union even refused to accept $10 notes in their pay packets. And so, in 1968, the CSIRO embarked on a 20-year project to create a more secure banknote.

POLYMER BANKNOTE

It was polymer scientist David Solomon, one of nine top scientists appointed to the project, who realised a plastic banknote might be the solution to the Reserve Bank's woes. By 1972, development of polymer banknotes had commenced and, after many delays, the first $10 polymer bank notes were issued in 1988, Australia's bicentennial year. They were worth the wait: the security features of a polymer banknote include watermarks, embossing, magnetic features embedded in the note and a transparent plastic window containing a diffractive 'Optically Variable Device' (OVD), a device that changes when held at different angles, in different lighting or exposed to different temperatures.

Now, 29 countries use polymer banknotes, both for their security features and for their durability. It's yet another example of how Australian ingenuity has helped solve some of the world's most vexing problems. The further one delves into the history of significant scientific inventions, the more one appreciates just how much Australian scientists, doctors and engineers have done to make our everyday lives that little bit less irritating (if you put a paper banknote through the wash, there's no happy ending).

We often struggle to articulate why it is that we are so proud to be Australian ('err ... mateship ... beaches ... fair go'). But our collection of very competent brains, so many of them nurtured by the CSIRO, is one of the very best reasons to love our country.

PACEMAKER

In the grand scheme of things, it doesn't matter much if you don't make it to the party, the office or the airport on time. It *does*, unfortunately, matter quite a lot if your heart is not on time.

Pacemaker

Humans have been fascinated by the function of the heart since they first became aware that this thumping thing in the centre of their chests was what kept them alive. In the 18th century, medical researchers began to realise there was electrical activity in the heart and embarked on a series of nutty experiments unlikely to pass muster with university ethics committees today. For example, in the late 1790s, French medical researcher Marie Francois Xavier Bichat used the country's surplus of guillotined heads to demonstrate that the human heart can still beat, *sans head*, if electrical currents are administered.

Mercifully, no decapitated bodies were required when Australian Dr Mark C. Lidwill invented the world's first artificial pacemaker in 1926. Lidwill's device, created with the help of physicist Edgar Booth, used electrical impulses to regulate the beating of the heart. The device was first used in 1928 to save the life of an infant born in cardiac arrest. The child's heart began beating by itself again after 10 minutes on the pacemaker. Prior to this, only artificial respiration and injections of adrenalin into the heart had been used to resuscitate the human heart.

Interestingly, Lidwill did not wish to be named as the inventor of the device, owing to the religious beliefs at the time that regarded any interference with the brain or heart as sacrilegious. The records of his invention were left with his lawyer and were destroyed after his death in 1969 at the age of 90. The baby that Lidwill saved in 1928 went on to recover completely and lead a healthy life, and ever-evolving incarnations of Lidwill's machine have helped saved countless lives, making him one of our greatest, if quietest, scientific achievers.

WARWICK CAPPER

When I recently checked into an ageing budget hotel with hints of a more extravagant 1980s past, I was struck by one thought: this looks like somewhere Warwick Capper would bring a Caloundra hairdresser for a one-night stand. You see, Warwick creeps into my thoughts whenever I'm in the vicinity of a little decayed '80s Aussie glamour.

Warwick Capper, the celebrity, is the genius invention of the Australian man himself, Warwick Capper.

Capper represents all that makes the '80s such rich fodder for the amateur and professional smart-arse: the hair (spiked mega-mullet soaring heavenwards, like a bogan cockatiel's); that *Penthouse* spread (Warwick and matchy-matchy then-wife Joanne, nude, *front on*); the clothes (teeny tiny shorts, budgie-smugglers, animal print for days); the pop single 'I Only Take What's Mine'; the pink Lamborghini.

WARWICK CAPPER

A quick recap for those who were little more than a glimmer in their parents' eye in 1985: in the '80s, Capper was a megawatt star in the AFL (or VFL, as it was known back then); a rare glittering poodle in a game not generally known for producing popstar porn actors. That's right – in 2009, Capper sold a home-made porno of him and his then girlfriend Kirsty to an adult film distributor for a six-figure sum. Pre-porn, Capper's footy career spanned 124 games and even more cans of Elnet hairspray. He played for the Sydney Swans before moving to the Brisbane Bears (now Lions) and was famed for his high-flying marks, as well being the highest earner in the game at the time, pulling $350,000 for a three-year contract with the Bears in 1987.

But who cares about that?! Warwick attained his legendary status mostly because, even for the '80s, he seemed to be taking the whole excess business a little too far. Embracing all the flashiest elements of the era, Capper took them to the next level and made them his own. Since his retirement from footy in 1991, his career has been a prolonged exercise in self-celebration. Capper's childlike eagerness and optimism seem to protect him from self-doubt and regret – a timider man might retreat into the shadows, bruised by one too many mocking headlines, but Capper gamely has worked as a stripper, an escort, a meter maid and a council worker, and has fronted large promotional campaigns for Nando's and quickbeds.com ('for hotels that are cheap and easy, like me').

As befits a reality TV contestant with a history of monetising his sex life, Capper shows real skill in assuming everyone loves his penis as much as he does. In 2002, he was booted from the *Celebrity Big Brother* house for exposing his gear to fellow housemates, a wake-up call that prompted him to go straight and open a chain of Evangelical churches. I'm kidding, of course. Capper continues to ride the celebrity guest speaker circuit, turning up to any event that can afford his fee. It's not too steep, either – and Nan's 80th is coming up ...

PENICILLIN

Now, I don't want to be the bearer of bad news, but you're not the most important Australian ever born. How do I know this? Because you're not Howard Walter Florey, and he died in 1968.

Florey was once described by Australia's longest-serving prime minister, Sir Robert Menzies, as 'the most important man ever born in Australia'. Florey found a way to turn the properties of penicillin into an effective drug – one that is estimated to have saved at least 200 million lives worldwide. Prior to the drug's introduction, it was not unusual to die from bacterial infections, often caused by nothing more than a simple scratch. A world without penicillin would be a world in which, frankly, there would be a lot more dead people.

Sir Alexander Fleming has long received the lion's share of credit for discovering penicillin and it *was* Fleming who in 1928 first observed that mould inhibited the growth of bacteria. Despite multiple experiments, though, Fleming was unable to find a way of purifying the compound and the discovery was not pursued again until 10 years later, when Florey, working with a small team of scientists, began investigating the properties of antibacterial substances produced by mould. Ernst Chain, one of the

PENICILLIN

team's members, found an article about Fleming's work in a medical journal and from here Florey and his team began to focus their efforts on turning the bacteria-inhibiting mould into a safe and effective drug.

By 1940, Florey and his team were ready to perform what would later be considered one of the most important medical experiments in history. Eight mice were injected with a lethal dose of streptococci bacteria. Four mice were given penicillin, four were not. The fortunate four treated with penicillin recovered fully and the untreated mice were dead within one day. Shortly after, Florey trialled the drug for the first time on a human. In 1941, a man named Albert Alexander became gravely ill after incurring a scratch from a rose in his garden. After receiving a dose of penicillin, Alexander began to recover, but Florey was unable to produce enough of the drug and Albert Alexander died. Shaken, Florey began tirelessly pursuing opportunities to produce the drug on a large scale, eventually finding assistance from the US Government. By the end of World War II in 1945, many laboratories were manufacturing penicillin and the lives of thousands of sick and wounded allied soldiers had been saved due to the drug.

Penicillin is now considered one of the ten most important medical discoveries of all time. But Florey didn't become a billionaire on the back of his hard work, as patenting the drug was considered medically unethical – a notion that now seems sadly antiquated. He was awarded numerous honours including a Nobel Prize for Physiology or Medicine (shared with Sir Alexander Fleming and Sir Ernst Boris Chain).

Florey was always humble about his momentous achievements and described his remarkable work as 'a terrible amount of luck'. Without Florey's 'terrible luck', though, many lives would be simply terrible.

BLACK BOX FLIGHT RECORDER

Unlike, say, hair in a can, scratch-n-sniff jeans or the selfie arm (a selfie stick in the shape of a human arm, so you can pretend someone else took your selfie) it's difficult to imagine anyone could file the black box into the 'stupid invention' category.

Hard as it may be to fathom, the black box was met with a shrug in the mid-1950s. Research scientist David Warren's interest in developing an in-flight recording device stemmed from his work investigating the crash of the world's first jet-powered commercial aircraft, the Comet, in 1953. Inspired by a miniature recorder he'd seen at a trade fair, Warren began working on a recording device for aircraft that would continuously record all the details of the flight and provide a record for investigators in the event of a crash.

BLACK BOX FLIGHT RECORDER

No one showed much interest in the recorder until a former British air vice-marshal, Sir Robert Hardingham, visited Warren's workplace, the Aeronautical Research Laboratory in Melbourne. Realising that Warren's invention had the potential to revolutionise the investigation of aviation accidents, Hardingham shipped Warren and his black box off to England in 1958, where both received a warm reception. The UK Ministry of Aviation promptly announced that in-flight recording devices were likely to become mandatory in the near future.

However, it was not until a Fokker Friendship plane owned by Trans Atlantic Airways (TAA) crashed in Mackay in 1960, killing all 29 passengers on board, that Australian authorities began to show an interest in the black box, with the inquiry judge in the case strongly recommending installation of in-flight recorders in all aircraft. After all but ignoring Warren's invention during the 1950s, in the early '60s Australia became the first country in the world to make cockpit voice recording mandatory. It would have doubtlessly been a proud moment for Warren, who, at nine years of age, lost his father in a plane crash over Bass Strait.

David Warren's invention has provided accident investigators with an invaluable tool for determining the cause of aeroplane crashes and helping prevent their recurrence. It is now mandatory for all major aircraft worldwide to install voice and data recording and in the past 40 years 100,000 flight recorders have been fitted on commercial aircraft. Flying is now safer than at any time in history and it is thanks in no small part to an Australian guy born on an island off the coast of the Northern Territory.

David Warren died in 2010 at the age of 85 in Melbourne. He was buried in a casket labelled 'Flight Recorder Inventor; Do not open', proving that scientific genius need not come at the expense of a good sense of humour.

ULTRASOUND
SCANNER

If you are pregnant but have no ultrasound picture of the baby to post on Facebook are you *really* pregnant? Thanks to two Australian men, this is a philosophical question you will never have to ask yourself.

In the late 1950s, concern about the use of X-rays in prenatal testing and their possible effects on the fetus was gathering pace. At the time, Australia's Commonwealth Acoustic Laboratories (CAL) had begun investigating recently emerged evidence that suggested images of developing fetuses could be safely produced using high-frequency soundwaves. In 1961, CAL scientists David Robinson and George Kossoff built the first ultrasound scanner, but it wasn't until 1962 that physicians conducted their first obstetrics exam with the scanner.

Ultrasound scanner

While the technology had been used in other parts of the world, Robinson and Kossoff's machine made much higher quality pictures than any other machine at the time. The superiority of their images subsequently put Australia far ahead of most other countries experimenting with the technology. The machine of 1962 was marginally more cumbersome than the ones used by today's specialists, requiring two circus strongmen to move it from room to room.*

Ultrasound scanners, put very simply, use sound beyond the limits of human hearing to take images using echolocation, a process where sound is bounced off an object to reveal its shape and position. No, it doesn't really make sense to me either, but that doesn't matter: the invention of the ultrasound scanner revolutionised medical imaging, and is now an indispensable tool in helping to diagnose problems in the abdomen, chest and reproductive organs. Robinson and Kossoff, using their machine, pioneered the way ultrasound would be used to detect fetal abnormalities, and it is thanks to their work that pregnancy and birth is now far less dangerous for women the world over – and far easier to share with 550 close personal friends on social media.

* Not really, but you get the idea.

Bionic Ear

In 1978, Dr Graeme Clark became the first person in the world to install a multi-channel cochlear implant, also known as a bionic ear. Motivated in part by his own father's diagnosis of severe, progressive deafness as a young man, Clark grew up wanting to 'fix people ears', as he put it. This motivation led to Clark almost single-handedly leading the race against the Americans and Europeans to build the bionic ear.

Bionic Ear

The idea of a 'bionic ear' came to Clark when he read a scientific paper from the US describing how a profoundly deaf person was able to receive hearing sensations through electrical stimulation, but not speech understanding. At the time, Clark was working as an ear surgeon in Melbourne and, spurred by the findings of the US paper, began researching the viability of an electronic implantable device.

It was a lonely and difficult journey and Clark spent years immersed in research and development. Funding for the project was scant and in Clark's own words, he was forced to 'rattle tins' and appear on telethons to raise funds. He was ridiculed and dismissed by colleagues, who believed a bionic ear was pie-in-the-sky stuff. The inner ear, they said, was just too complicated. One prominent ear surgeon described Clark as a 'clown'.

The challenge of fitting electrodes into the tiny inner ear was significant but Clark was determined to prove his critics wrong: 'In spite of the problems and criticisms, I just had to go on. A cochlear implant was their only hope of ever hearing', he said.

Today, hundreds of thousands of profoundly deaf children and adults have received a cochlear implant from Clark's organisation, Cochlear Limited. If you've ever seen a video of a deaf child reacting to hearing for the first time, you'll completely understand why Clark claims he never tires of seeing that reaction. Of that first successful multi-channel cochlear implant in 1978, Clark has said: 'When he heard his first words I was just so overcome I went into the next door laboratory and wept for joy.' It is a moment of pure wonder, guaranteed to get the tear ducts in a tizzy – and it's all because of the relentless dedication of one Australian man.

BOOMERANG

Some inventions get more attention than they deserve. The Thermomix, for example, which is just a big dumb rice cooker with a hilarious price tag, yields more than 25 million Google search results. Yet enter 'Australian boomerang' and a middling 520,000 results appear. This, folks, is berserk. The boomerang, which has been used by Indigenous Australians for tens of thousands of years, is an aerodynamic hunting tool that can kill a kangaroo *and* return itself to its thrower along a parabolic flight path *even when thrown in space*. Can your Thermomix do *that*?

BOOMERANG

Despite its comparatively paltry Google results, the boomerang is widely regarded as one of man's greatest inventions. It has the same characteristics as a bird's wing – that is, the upper surface is greater than the surface underneath. In aviation speak, that's known as an aerofoil, or a surface that's designed to lift with the help of air currents.

In 1914, South Australian Ngarrindjeri man David Unaipon conceptualised the helicopter based on the principal of boomerang flight. Unaipon, commemorated on our $50 note, was fascinated with the concept of perpetual motion. He also invented a sheep-shearing handpiece, a centrifugal motor, a multi-radial wheel and a mechanical propulsion device, yet never received any financial support to develop his ideas. Aboriginal people had begun sowing the seeds of our reputation for world-first innovations long before Unaipon's time though; well before any other societies, they started sharpening edges on their cutting tools, and using stone to grind up seeds.

Boomerangs were used by Aboriginal people primarily for hunting, with different boomerangs used for different purposes. On the New South Wales coast, for example, lighter boomerangs made from mangroves were used for duck hunting. In desert areas, heavier wood from the mulga tree was used for boomerangs designed to hunt kangaroos. The carvings and colouring of boomerangs also varied widely throughout regions and in the Aboriginal Dreamtime myths, many significant features of our landscape – rock formations, rivers and mountains – were created by ancestors throwing boomerangs and spears into the earth.

The boomerang is regarded by Aboriginal people as a symbol of the strength of their culture and depictions of boomerangs being used to hunt animals appear in rock art in the Kimberley that's been dated back as far as 20,000 years. You might not be able to make risotto with it, but the boomerang is an enduring example of the incredible skill and ingenuity of Aboriginal people.

Dual-flush toilet

I bet you haven't spent too much time pondering your dual-flush toilet. Yet, every day, you, the dual-flush toilet user, get to solve your own floating riddle: will 3 litres of water deliver this baby to the sewer? Or is it more of a 6-litre job? As a risk-free form of scatological Russian roulette, it's not too shabby. The worst outcome is nothing more dangerous than a stubborn floater.

Given we're a nation that's made a cultural icon of the dunny, and never frowns at a poo-joke, it's hardly surprising that the dual-flush toilet is an Australian invention. In 1980, Bruce Thompson, an employee of South Australian bathroom brand Caroma, developed a cistern with two buttons that corresponded with two different flush volumes. By pressing either a half flush or full flush button, users could decide how much water was needed to finish the job. Thompson developed his invention with the help of a $130,000 government grant in a rare example of taxpayer money *literally* being flushed down the toilet, and for a worthy cause to boot. It wasn't Caroma's first successful loo experiment, either. Nearly 40 years earlier, in 1941, company founder Charles Rothauser had invented the world's first all-plastic, one-piece moulded cistern.

Initial trials of the dual-flush toilet began in a small town in South Australia and the water-saving benefits were immediately apparent: the average household saved a whopping 32,000 litres of water per year. For Australia, being the driest inhabited continent on earth, the dual-flush toilet proved a painless way of conserving precious water. Following the success of initial trials, legislation in every state but New South Wales made it compulsory for all new buildings to install dual-flush toilets.

The dual-flush is now shipped to more than 30 countries worldwide, keen to adopt a system that saves about 51 litres of water per person per day, compared to

Dual-flush toilet

a single-flush cistern. Interestingly, Germany, despite a long history of innovation, was one of the few countries to poo-poo the dual-flush toilet and to this day remains steadfastly committed to its horrifying shelf toilets. For those lucky enough not to have pooed in Germany, the shelf toilet lets the poo fall onto a dry 'viewing platform', rather than straight into water for flushing. The maker of the poo is thus able to scrutinise their work in the manner of a coroner examining a body on a slab.

Thank-you, Bruce Thompson, for giving us the eco-friendly dual-flush option. If you'd invented the shelf toilet, our thanks would be somewhat less sincere.

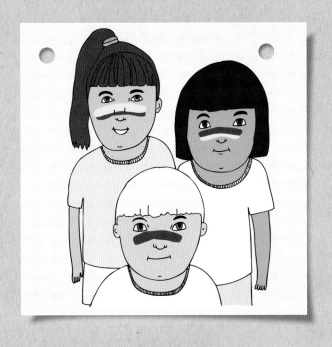

AUSTRALIAN WAY OF LIFE

Very expensive housing

Mwahahahaha. Do you hear that? That's the sound of Lucifer laughing gleefully at the havoc and heartbreak he has wrought upon Australian home buyers. Or it could just be the sound of another real estate agent pocketing his latest commission – it's hard to tell the difference sometimes.

Once upon a time, if you wanted to buy a house in Australia, all you needed, essentially, was to have a job. It didn't need to be a fancy job, either. Anyone with full-time work and the willpower to refrain from spending all their earnings on West Coast Coolers and Contiki tours could buy a house.

Very expensive housing

In 1978, the median house price in Melbourne was $37,600. In 2016, 38 years later, Melbourne's median house price was $795,447 (there's that laughter in the background again!). It's even worse in Sydney, which has the downright offensive median of $1.12 million. Then there's Brisbane ($540,758), Adelaide ($501,166), Darwin ($591,167), Canberra ($684, 395) and Perth ($573, 766). Only Hobart offers a median house price below half a million, at $382, 888 and steadily climbing.

But that's OK. At least it's still cheap to *rent* a house, right? Well, no. Anyone who has ever tried to secure an affordable rental property within striking distance – and increasingly, *not* within striking distance – of the centre of a major Australian metropolis will know that 'affordable rental property' and 'major Australian metropolis' are mutually exclusive.

You know things are bad when articles start appearing in your newsfeed with headlines like 'Which nightmare Sydney housing horror scenario is right for you?' (an actual domain.com.au headline from April 2017). So then, let's have a look at what kind of digs a single person on a disability or unemployment pension in the Sydney and Illawarra area could afford. The answer is – nothing! That's right, nothing. This sobering fact was turned up by a 2017 Anglicare study into affordable housing, which found that 'there are now zero affordable options in the Sydney-Illawarra area for single people on unemployment and disability pensions'.

Let's say you're a little more fortunate and have $600 a week to spend on rent – a healthy amount by anyone's measure. In inner Sydney, that will get you a one-bedroom flat in a block that might have its charms, but may just as likely be entirely void of them. You want a house? Marry a Murdoch – or move to Millicent in South Australia, just a 30-minute drive from Mount Gambier. There, $190 a week will get you a decent three-bedder and $245 will get you a bright and airy, renovated four-bedroom house.

Millicent, we'll see you soon – just as soon as we've saved enough petrol money after paying the rent. Should only take three years.

MULTICULTURALISM

Australia, you are good at lots of things, but pronouncing ethnic last names is not one of them. If it's more complicated than 'Jones', you are probably going to mangle it. Asian migrants have long recognised this, with many anglicising their names on arrival to avoid the repetitive strain of pronouncing their name 50 times a day.

Crap pronunciation aside, multiculturalism has been a resounding success. Australia's policy on multiculturalism, adopted in the 1970s, was designed to endorse and celebrate cultural diversity. The White Australia policy had taken an assimilationist approach, meaning that migrants were expected to drop any vestiges of their ethnic background and language when they arrived. By 1975, politicians at both ends of the political spectrum recognised the failures and inherent unfairness of this policy and began to rewrite the book on immigration. The Australian Ethnic Affairs Council, appointed to advise the Fraser government, recommended a public policy of multiculturalism, and in 1978 Australia's first official multicultural policies were implemented.

While vigorous debate about the pros and cons of multiculturalism is an ongoing feature of our media landscape, a 2015 Mapping Social Cohesion survey found that 86 per cent of Australians agree that multiculturalism has been good for the country. That's a pretty hefty majority for whom the debate has already been decided.

It's impossible to imagine Australia without cultural diversity, simply because so much of our everyday life is shaped by the contributions of migrants. In most of our capital cities, you can get up in the morning and buy olives and pasta from a Mediterranean wholesaler, Ayurvedic toothpaste at an Indian grocery, pastries from a Turkish bakery and sushi from the Japanese girls down the road. Get your boots fixed by a Chilean shoemaker and while you wait, order a coffee made with an espresso machine

MULTICULTURALISM

introduced to the country by Italian migrants. For lunch, you can eat spongy injera bread and a curry at an Ethiopian restaurant, or mee goreng at an Indonesian restaurant. After lunch, get your clothes altered by a Vietnamese seamstress and buy dressmaking fabric from a Transylvanian émigré – who will probably be my father because, let's face it, there aren't that many Transylvanian fabric wholesalers. Duck into the market and buy a chicken for Sunday dinner from a Hungarian and get your eyebrows threaded by an Iranian woman. Finally, go home to your house built by Macedonians, for a meeting with your Maltese accountant to do your taxes.

And you can be sure that you *won't* sit down for a dinner of tripe in white sauce. Thank God for cultural diversity.

Deni Ute Muster

Wikipedia defines a ute muster as: 'an Australian festival which brings together large numbers of utes and their owners. These events typically include competitions and other side events, occur annually, and normally last several days and are held in rural and regional areas of Australia and New Zealand.'

While accurate, this doesn't really give a sense of what it's like to experience Australia's premier ute event, the Deni Ute Muster, held each year at Deniliquin in New South Wales' Riverina area. Based on Wikipedia's description, you might think it was just

AUSTRALIAN WAY OF LIFE

Deni Ute Muster

a group of sedate car aficionados admiring each other's modifications before retiring to the CWA tent for scones and tea. But the reality is closer to what one journalist described as 'Burning Man for bogans'.

The basic premise of the festival is celebrating and admiring utes, but the Deni Ute Muster is much more than a car show. There's also whip-cracking championships, monster trucks, wood-chopping contests and a slew of awards like 'best country ute', 'best town ute', 'best chick's ute' and 'best tradie's ute' to be won. There's even a blue singlet count (the current record stands at 3959 blue singlets).

The success of the Deni Ute Muster is hard to overstate, but Deniliquin has given it a good stab by impaling a giant ute on a pole in the town's centre. Once known primarily for merino wool, Deniliquin is now 'the official ute capital of the world', with Paris coming a close second (jokes, jokes).

The Deni Ute Muster took place for the first time on 2 October 1999, immediately gaining a place in the *Guinness Book of Records* for the largest parade of legally registered utes in the world. The muster now attracts big-ticket performers like Keith Urban and Cold Chisel and draws crowds upwards of 20,000. Yet, ask a city dweller what they know about Deniliquin and they'll likely respond with a blank, 'Denili ... what?'.

The Deni Ute Muster is a true celebration of regional Australia in all its dusty, unhinged glory. Despite some questionable behaviour – drinking beer drip-fed through a woman's cleavage, men flopping their gear out at the suggestion of a photographer's lens, nudie discos, mud wrestling – crime is rarely an issue. Given the enormous quantities of booze consumed during the festival, the lack of crime and violence is both surprising and a testament to the good-natured, high-spirited personalities of the festival-goers. City dwellers should be so lucky.

HILLS HOIST

So you think the Hills Hoist is just a clothesline? Have you never eaten a donut strung from a Hills Hoist at a birthday party? Or held on for dear life as your older sister tries to make you fall off and cry as she spins you in circles? Or choked back cheap wine in a friendly game of Goon of Fortune (see pg. 115)?

Technically the Hills Hoist *is* just a rotary clothesline, and not even the first one, but two things make it special: it was the first truly affordable clothesline and it was the first to feature a crown-and-pinion mechanism for raising and lowering the line, an essential design feature for enabling small kids to grab on and go for a dizzying whizz around.

AUSTRALIAN WAY OF LIFE

HILLS HOIST

In 1945, motor mechanic Lance Hill invented his famous clothesline in his Adelaide shed after he returned home from World War II. Lance's wife, Sherry, had been complaining that their clothesline, strung between two posts, was in the way of the lemon tree, and given the amount of domestic slavery that was expected of a woman in this era, you can well imagine how a poorly placed clothesline might have induced apoplectic rage.

The first batch of Hills Hoists were made with metal tubing salvaged from the anti-submarine boom net that hung under the Sydney Harbour Bridge during World War II. They were an immediate hit with Lance's friends and family. The enthusiastic response prompted Lance and his brother-in-law, Harold Ling, to establish a business, Hills, to keep up with the demand, which was growing at lightning speed. They eventually had to purchase salvaged army trucks to cope with the volume of deliveries. By 1994, five million Hills Hoists had been sold, which goes some way to explaining why they loom so large in the childhood memories of Australians.

In 1996, to mark the first 50 years of the Hills company, the Adelaide Festival of Arts chose a Hills Hoist, held high like a torch, to promote its program around the world. But the Hills Hoist's status as a universally recognised symbol of Australian life was *really* broadcast to the world when it appeared in the Sydney 2000 Olympics opening ceremony with flames shooting out of it, just like your one at home! Today, there's a Hills Hoist on display at the Sydney Powerhouse Museum.

In 2017, it was announced that Hills, which long ago branched into other household items, had sold the rights to their most famous product. But not to worry – Aussie kids will still be whizzing around the Hills Hoist for years to come as the new owners have said they will continue to manufacture them. If that's not reason enough for a celebratory game of Goon of Fortune, what is?

ODD ROAD SIGNS

Don't you just hate it when your car gets eaten by a cow, or worse, when a kangaroo seizes your car and lifts it up by the bonnet? Luckily, these scenarios, which, let's face it, we've all experienced on the road at one stage or another, are easily avoided if you just pay attention to the signs. Literally. Australia has a disproportionately high number of singularly odd road signs, with graphics that often depict a scenario markedly stranger than the one they are attempting to warn you about. There are no car-snacking cows in Australia, as far as I can tell. But there are cows that cross roads, and therefore are at risk of being hit by cars. Ditto for the strongman kangaroo.

Of course, in a country as ripe with natural hazards as Australia, signs are often a life-saving necessity, and not just for roos and cows. Most visitors to the Northern Territory, for example, would finish their holiday in a body bag were it not for the signs around rivers, lakes, and waterholes warning of crocodiles. Warning signs about jellyfish are also a common sight on North Queensland beaches. Some of them even attempt to demonstrate what an encounter with a stinger actually *looks* like, and let's just say it's doubtful any actual victims were consulted during the design process. One such example in Queensland reads 'Marine stingers are present in these waters during the summer months' and is accompanied by a graphic of an amorous jellyfish that appears to be softly caressing a swimmer with its tentacles. In turn, the swimmer appears to execute a balletic motion with his legs, presumably to indicate extreme pain rather than an underwater rehearsal of *Swan Lake*. It is unintentionally beautiful and almost makes an encounter with an Irukandji jellyfish look like something you might actually want to experience on your Australian adventure, just after you've ticked off climbing the Harbour Bridge and cuddling a koala.

Odd road signs

Even more questionable is the need for signs that caution against interrupting copulating kangaroos, because obviously that's what most people are tempted to do every time they see two marsupials mid-coitus. Helpfully, the sign depicts one kangaroo mounting another, in case you were in any doubt as to what kangaroo sex looks like. And let's not think too long about what circumstances led to the need for a sign on South Australia's Fleurieu Peninsula that warns motorists *not to run over baby penguins in their cars*. Honestly, Australia! Do you really need to be told not to run over baby penguins? What next? A sign that warns against adding newborns to your bone broth?

Zinc-smeared faces

Residing in an area that naturally receives large amounts of UV radiation *and* sits directly under a depleted section of the ozone layer means Australians are obliged to make peace with two incontrovertible facts: a) they will age faster than their European friends, most likely resembling a piece of battered carry-on luggage by the time they're 40; and b) when it comes to protecting their skin against premature ageing and skin cancer, a discreet coat of delicate SPF 15 is not going to do the trick.

Zinc, that thick white paste that makes you look a bit like you've smeared pigeon poo on your face, is one of the only foolproof ways to guard against being accidentally put on the baggage belt at the airport. Don't like the white cast it leaves on your face? Neither do kids. In fact, kids deplore most forms of sun protection and would sooner endure full-body blistering rather than consent to five minutes of rigorous sunscreen application.

Enter coloured zinc.

Australian kids grow up believing it's perfectly normal to swipe garishly coloured zinc cream over their noses and lips. They wear it at swimming carnivals to show their team colours, at the beach in whatever colours take their fancy, and they wear it when their Mum won't let them watch TV and there's nothing else to do except experiment with their own faces, in a way that will inevitably lead to staining of the 'good couch'. Coloured zinc is thrillingly lurid, giving the wearer the nuclear neon hue of one who has just been injected with strontium-90.

Aesthetics aside, the kids are onto something. Zinc oxide has been used since 500 BC to treat wounds and skin conditions. It's used in nappy rash and antiseptic

Zinc-smeared faces

creams, but perhaps its greatest strength lies in its ability to protect our skin from the sun. Chemical sunscreens work by changing UV rays into heat, and then releasing that heat from the skin. Zinc oxide sits on top of the skin and reflects the sun's rays off, making it an actual physical block between them and your skin. There is no better way to guard your skin against the savagery of the Australian sun, barring locking yourself indoors with the blinds drawn, which pretty much rules out every sacred Australian leisure activity except binge drinking.

The lesson here? Sometimes, the kids really do know best.

Talking about what it means to be Australian

You know those people who are only interested in the conversation if it's about them? Australia is a bit like those people. We love an opinion piece here, a panel show there, about 'what it means to be Australian'. And, boy, do we love to hear what foreign visitors think of us. If you're an international comedian fronting up to the land down under for the first time, here's a pro tip: just talk to the audience about how Australians are super chilled out, how quaint and droll and singular we are. Swear a lot, too. They will love you, probably more than your audience back home does.

Talking about what it means to be Australian

Australia likes to hear funny things about itself – and, preferably, *nice* things. A likely explanation is our geographical isolation. We live so far from absolutely everyone else on the planet that it's hard to know if the rest of the world even knows we exist, let alone has an opinion on us. *Aliens* live closer to Europe than we do. If we want to know what other countries think of us, we can't do as the Brits do and jump on the Eurostar, get served a croissant by a rude waiter in Paris and be reminded that the French still hate us. No, if *we* want to know if people hate us, we have to clamber aboard a plane and fly till our ankles are so swollen they could support a freeway overpass. Consequently, we gobble it up when someone makes the effort to fly all the way over here to throw around a few gags about utes, thongs and mozzies.

All this need for validation and self-examination can get a bit pathetic, though, like a child who needs to be told that every scribbled stick figure is a work of blazing genius. Australia, you are OK! People from other countries envy our beaches, sunshine, very attractive people (we really are adorable) and lack of war and strife. WE ARE OK.

But ...? But ...? But – what *does* it mean to be Australian? In a nutshell, it means living with lots of animals that scare the pants off foreign visitors, barbecuing anything that can be cooked, and enjoying the rich spoils of a peaceably multicultural society. It means being envied by many other less materially fortunate, majestically beautiful and seasonally varied countries. It means that, by the time you are four years old, you might've lived under the same number of prime ministers as your age.

Still, a pat on the head never hurts one's self-esteem. When is Arj Barker next in town?

BIRDS

Have you ever thought about how extraordinary it is that we live in a country where magpie attacks are such a common occurrence? There is no other country in the world in which it is casually accepted that magpies will attempt to gouge out your eyes as you ride your bike to work.

And make no mistake, the magpie does not want to scare you, it wants to *hurt* you. According to Griffith University's Darryl Jones, an expert in magpie behaviour, one school in Brisbane endured a lengthy period of terror courtesy of a demonic magpie, which cut the faces of 100 students during its reign of blood. School drop-offs resembled an episode of *Game of Thrones*, with parents screaming at their children to run as fast as they could across the oval and into the main building of the school, where the school nurse waited, ready to treat casualties.

Birds

This stuff doesn't happen in England and Germany, even though they have magpies of their own. Australian magpies have been described as the most aggressive urban bird in the world. Dr Jones even wrote a book, *Magpie Alert,* devoted solely to the subject of magpie attacks – a book that could only have been published in Australia.

European settlers loathed our birds. They feared the squawking racket could have a barbarous effect on the Australian people, fretting that without the soothing sound of European birdsong, their souls would wither. Clearly, they were homesick, but they also weren't imagining things. Australian birds are quite simply the loudest and most aggressive birds on the planet. But they're also the most intelligent and that's because they have been on the planet longer than any other birds on Earth. Every single birdsong in the world is descended from Australian ancestors, according to scientist Tim Low, author of *Where Song Began*. Sixty million years of evolution has taught these birds lessons that their much younger European counterparts are yet to learn, like kidnapping, and screeching at the top of their lungs while nice people try to buy rhubarb at the farmers market.

The bizarre and aggressive behaviour of Australian birds is partly due to the fact that the Australian landscape is dominated by eucalypt trees. Eucalypts, unlike most European trees, are pollinated by birds, not wind, meaning that nectar is easily accessible and highly visible. Birds don't need to be smart to find it; they just need to be rambunctious and rude. It's a bit like the Boxing Day sales.

They may be bombastic, but Australian birds are also the most interesting on the planet. Katharine Hepburn certainly thought so, becoming so bewitched by the sounds of lyrebirds in Sherbrooke Forest, just outside Melbourne, that while in town she visited them every day to see what her biographer described as 'a thrilling, rib-tingling experience, like a sexual, exciting play'. Australian lyrebirds are also capable of replicating the somewhat less erotic sound of a chainsaw gang. Do you need any more motivation to look up next time you hear a kerfuffle in the trees above you?

PRETENTIOUS COFFEE

A short story about coffee by someone who has never set foot in Australia:

> Coffee is a hot drink made from coffee beans. There are two ways to drink coffee – with milk or without. You drink it in the morning to wake you up and sometimes in the afternoon to wake you up again. You shouldn't drink it at night, as it will wake you up.
>
> The end.

After you've stopped rolling around the floor in mirth and wiped the tears of hilarity from your face, you may want to consider the sobering fact that for many people around the world, that is simply all there is to say about coffee. Australians on the other hand – I'm looking at you, Melbourne – decided that the making of a cup of coffee should be as complex as an IVF embryo transfer, and almost as expensive.

Ordering a coffee in Melbourne – and increasingly every Australian city, town and rural village – requires an encyclopaedic knowledge of the various ways in which the coffee bean can be manipulated. Flat white, long black with half a sugar, cold drip, skinny decaf latte, the options seem endless! To say we have a love affair with coffee would be an understatement; it's more of a deranged obsession. Coffee is a gateway into a world of one-upmanship and snootery. Don't even get me started on the milk options (half-fat, soy, almond milk, coconut milk ...).

Twenty years ago, most Australians were happy chugging down cups of International Roast, with its top notes of industrial-strength processing chemicals. The slippery seeds of addiction were sewn by Italian migrants, who brought the first espresso machines into the country in the mid-1950s. By the 1990s, we were starting to pay attention to their more sophisticated treatment of the bean: 'Ohh, a latte! That sounds interesting',

PRETENTIOUS COFFEE

FRIGID
SLOW
WEEPING
CAFFEINE
PREPARATION

we said. Before too long, the latte became a short black, which became an espresso, which became a ristretto, which became a single-origin cold drip with condensed milk and whale sperm pearls – until, finally, it became THREE TEST TUBES OF DECONSTRUCTED COFFEE and we realised we'd hit rock bottom.

And now, here we are, as dependent on our coffee to keep us alive as we are on our lungs; hands permanently curved into wretched claws from clutching the takeaway cups we cling to like life rafts. Australia! Wake up and smell the coffee – you are a nation of addicts! (Oooh, is that a top note of honeysuckle I detect?)

ESKIES

PROBLEM: You would like to get stonkered at your mate's Sunday barbie, but the weather will be stinking, there's not a great deal of foliage in their backyard and they live a 45-minute drive from your house. How to keep the beers deliciously cold and refreshing? How to preserve that heat-busting crispness that signals the beginning of fun times?

SOLUTION: Australia's favourite portable pub, the Esky.

What a gift it is to not have to drink warm beer! With parts of Australia sweltering through summers above 40 degrees Celsius, this is no mean feat. The famed blue and white portable cooler – credited by some historians as the first of its kind in the world, and by its creators as 'the first *official* portable cooler in the world' – was made by a Sydney refrigeration company called Malley's in 1941. Malley's claims they created their first Esky ice box in 1884, but didn't start advertising it until 1941. This was not the Esky familiar to most Australians, but a compact fridge for homes. It's doubtless a source of perpetual annoyance to Malley's that 'esky' is now a generic term for any portable cooler, appropriated by many other manufacturers.

AUSTRALIAN WAY OF LIFE

ESKIES

But it was undeniably Malley's who, in 1952, gave us the portable Esky as we know it. The original model, an insulated box made from galvanised iron, could hold six one-pint (around 600 millilitre) bottles and also had three racks for food. It was the perfect invention for its time, when cars were starting to become a feature of everyday life and people could drive to the country for a picnic, and it became known as the car fridge.

It was claimed that by 1960, when Australia's population was about 10 million, 500,000 households owned an Esky. By that stage, the design had been improved to include a lock-down lid, which, frankly, could still use some improving (is there any object that can successfully contain the dripping juice of a watermelon?) – a bottle opener (sweet) and a hole for draining melted ice.

It has since assumed an important role in the lives of Australian beer drinkers, some of whom have gone so far as to customise their Eskies with motors and wheels. In case you had plans to do the same, it should be noted that the police take a dim view of Esky cars, and will not hesitate to fine the owners and impound the cooler.

In a nod to its significance in our ~~drinking~~ cultural landscape, organisers of the closing ceremony at the Sydney 2000 Olympic Games presented each attendee with a small polystyrene Esky.

So, next time you're choking down a warm beer at the beach because you didn't have time to clean the watermelon juice out of the Esky before you left the house, give your silent thanks to Malley's. Without them, you might never have experienced cold beer at the beach in the first place.

SLIP, SLOP, SLAP

Seagulls are crap. They're loud, intrusive, steal all your fish and chips and can really botch a sunset beach proposal. You wouldn't pick one to front a ginormous public health campaign about the dangers of skin cancer, would you?

Well, in 1981, someone in Ad Land did exactly that. Clad in board shorts, hat and T-shirt, Sid the Seagull dispensed sun-smart advice in a series of animated TV ads to a nation for whom in the '70s 'sun-smart' meant remembering to apply baby oil while basking in the sun.

Slip, slop, slap

In the ad's maddeningly catchy jingle, Sid implored us to:

Slip, Slop, Slap! It sounds like a breeze when you say it like that.
Slip, Slop, Slap! In the sun we always say Slip, Slop, Slap!
Slip, Slop, Slap!
Slip on a shirt, slop on sunscreen and slap on a hat
Slip, Slop, Slap! You can stop skin cancer – say: Slip, Slop, Slap!

And what do you know? We listened to the seagull. Sid's sun-smart message changed the way Australians looked at skin cancer and the danger of sun exposure. Children were unceremoniously forced into wide-brimmed school hats, with 'no hat, no play' becoming the policy of choice for schools battling pint-sized hat haters. The deep golden tan we all associated with health, attractiveness and the good life started to look markedly less appealing when we realised it could kill us. People started using SPF 5, which now seems quaintly inadequate, and rethought their old habit of using alfoil and coconut oil to help the suns rays to darken their pallor.

Since the introduction of the Slip, Slop, Slap campaign, the rates of the two most common forms of skin cancer have decreased, sun protection has become compulsory in all schools and childcare centres, and, between 1981 and 1991, rates of sunburn – a precursor to the formation of skin cancers – dropped by 50 per cent.

So, while the pesky, baby-munching seagull (they will eat their young if you don't throw enough fries their way) may be responsible for filching your grub at the beach, it's thanks to seagull Sid that Australians, who have the highest incidence of skin cancer of any country in the world, have learned to slip, slop, slap ourselves out of harm's way, and to use baby oil for its original intended purpose, which is, um, what exactly?

BUSHFIRES

Few aspects of Australian life are as feared and loathed as bushfires. We are the most flammable country on Earth and bushfires have been part of the Australian landscape for an estimated 60 million years – long enough for some of our native flora to have evolved to depend on fire for regeneration. Some plants have even developed fire-resistant seeds, or seeds that spiral into the ground when conditions are dry so they remain protected as bushfires tear through the surrounding environment.

AUSTRALIAN WAY OF LIFE

Bushfires

Unfortunately, humans are yet to develop a physiological defence against bushfires, but we are fortunate to have a large body of vigilant authorities watching our backs. Local authorities such as the Country Fire Authority (CFA) use radio, television and mass text messaging to alert residents to potential dangers. Federally, the Bureau of Meteorology (BOM) provides 'fire danger ratings' every day of the bushfire season, warning Australians of the level of fire risk in their area. The BOM overhauled its fire-danger ratings system in 2010 to include a new level of threat: 'catastrophic'. Terrible events preceded, and prompted, these changes.

Australian Bureau of Statistics found that Victoria has suffered significantly more fatalities from bushfires than anywhere else in the country. The state is considered one of the most fire-prone areas in the world and Victorians know all too well the sick dread induced by a 46-degree day with high winds. The Ash Wednesday bushfires, which hit Victoria and South Australia on 16 February 1983 claimed 75 lives.

But worse was to come for Victoria on 7 February 2009, a day now known as Black Saturday. A series of massive bushfires – the worst in Australia's history – tore through towns and national parks on the north-eastern outskirts of Melbourne, killing 173 people and destroying more than 2000 homes. It was after a Royal Commission into the Black Saturday bushfires that a raft of new fire-management strategies were implemented, including the BOM's revamped fire-danger ratings system.

Does Australia stand a chance of ever managing the bushfire threat? Pre-colonisation, the fire-planning methods of Aboriginal people dramatically reduced the reach and intensity of bushfires, helping to preserve delicate plant life in fire-prone areas. Returning to Aboriginal fire management may no longer be a realistic option, but adopting the principles of traditional burning might help reduce the damage wrought by major bushfires – and prevent any more days of the week earning an ominous prefix.

Second verse of the national anthem

Paradoxically, nothing says 'proud Australian' more than the inability to remember all the words to 'Advance Australia Fair'. The first verse is a cinch, hard-wired into the brains of all Australians thanks to the nocturnal activity of the Patriot Pixies, who visit every Australian man, woman and child while they sleep, whispering the words 'Australians all let us rejoice, for we are young and free...' into our ears until they're permanently embedded into our grey matter.

The Patriot Pixies obviously excused themselves for a smoko when it came to the second verse, though, leaving an entire nation in a spot of bother whenever called upon to mumble the anthem in its entirety.

You're probably trying to remember that second verse right now. Allow me to jog your memory. (Back in a sec; just got to google it.)

Beneath our radiant Southern Cross
We'll toil with hearts and hands;
To make this Commonwealth of ours
Renowned of all the lands;
For those who've come across the seas
We've boundless plains to share;
With courage let us all combine
To Advance Australia Fair.
In joyful strains then let us sing,
Advance Australia Fair.

Second verse of the national anthem

♫ BENEATH OUR...
... RADIANT ??? ♫

Perhaps we tune out because the second verse gets a bit killjoy, what with the toiling and all. As a nation with a proud and honourable history of bludging, slacking off and sickie-chucking, is anyone surprised we're not mad about that verse? The sentiments are generally commendable: *We've boundless plains to share; With courage let us all combine to Advance Australia Fair.* Nonetheless, we suffer from a kind of collective dementia when it comes to remembering the words.

Nowhere is this phenomenon more comically on display than at an AFL or NRL grand final, in which a bunch of dinky-di Aussie blokes deal with the embarrassment of fluffing the second verse by clamping their mouths shut and staring straight ahead, or moving their lips around as if searching for a pocket of oxygen that might magically render them invisible. Sub the footy players for any Olympic gold-medal winner, or any Australian really, and the results would be identical.

It is precisely *because* of our collective inability to remember the words that the second verse of 'Advance Australia Fair' binds us together like glue, a poignant reminder that, whatever our differences, we are united in apathy and indifference to the bit that begins with the words, 'Beneath our radiant Southern Cross' and ends in ... who cares?

Climate Extremes

Australian tourism campaigns tend to focus on the regions of Australia that enjoy year-round sunshine. If you've ever endured a Tasmanian winter, you'll understand why. 'Tasmania: bring a parka' doesn't have quite the same ring to it as 'Queensland: beautiful one day, perfect the next'. Similarly, Lara Bingle draped on a sunlounge on a beach is a marginally more seductive scenario than Anna from Launceston desperately scouring her local Target for a pair of woollen tights.

This is not to suggest the cooler regions of Australia aren't blessed with an abundance of charms; it's not their fault international tourists have been led to believe sleeves are a novelty item in Australia, a myth that's undone even the hardiest of British tourists. It's always fun watching underdressed tourists turning into human ice sculptures while taking in the sights. The only thing more fun is chatting about the weather, and no one can do it quite like Melburnians, who have a delightful tendency to be stunned by their own weather, no matter how many times they experience its notorious unpredictability.

CLIMATE EXTREMES

Sydneysiders have their own nonsensical weather behaviours, refusing to acknowledge that their city is not bathed in year-round sunshine and warmth. Visit Sydney in July and watch the locals feign surprise at the cryogenic conditions: 'Dunno what's up with this cold', they'll tell you, 'last week was all low-20s!'

Australia's variable climates are due to its small landmass in relation to the expanse of ocean that surrounds it and its position across temperate, tropical, and subtropical zones. These variations mean there is no one seasonal calendar that works for the whole continent; Australia is instead divided into six distinct climatic regions – tropical, equatorial, subtropical, grassland, temperate and desert. Even within one state, there may be multiple climate zones. Queensland, for instance, has all six climate zones represented within its boundaries.

It's easy to see why British tourists are often caught unawares by the insufficiency of their threads in Australia. In Britain, if it's winter, you will be cold, anywhere you go. In summer you probably will be, too. Dressing correctly for an Australia-wide adventure is a much darker art, requiring an almost clairvoyant ability to foresee what the weather will do. An itinerary that takes in Perth and Hobart in summer could see you experiencing temperatures as high as 40 degrees Celsius and as low as 3. If you add Melbourne to the mix, you might find yourself splashing around in a pool at 3pm and huddled up to a heater by 7pm, with drastic temperature changes of up to 20 degrees not uncommon.

We could do a lot to help tourists enjoy Australia more by pressuring our airlines to change the luggage allowances for incoming arrivals, to allow for the approximately 40 kilograms of clothing they'll need to see them through the various regions. A new climate awareness campaign to run alongside our Bingle-esque tourism ads wouldn't hurt either. How about: 'Australia: crematorium one day, cryogenic chamber the next'?

Mid-century homes

When we think of mid-century modernist architecture, we tend to think Palm Springs glamour and futurist glass boxes jutting out of the Hollywood Hills. So it may surprise you to learn Australia has a rich seam of innovative mid-century design running through its streets, and is home to some of the best examples of domestic modernist architecture in the world. The millionaire's enclave of Studley Park in Melbourne's Kew is the most concentrated pocket of modernist Australia, and Canberra also hosts a fine collection of lovingly preserved modernist architecture.

Mid-century homes

Australia faced a severe housing shortage following World War II. An influx of migrants and returned servicemen meant we needed 400,000 new homes – fast. The results were initially less than inspiring. The bungalows of the 1930s and '40s, adorned with eaves, verandahs and fireplaces, were now too expensive to build, so by the early '50s, boxy, uninspiring double- and triple-fronted brick homes had become the norm. It wasn't until modernist architects like Robin Boyd, Anatol Kagan, Harry Seidler and Pettit+Sevitt came along with a different vision of suburban living that we started to break the monotony of postwar housing. Their optimistic reimagining of what domestic life could look like changed the way we live.

Got an open-plan kitchen/living/dining area? Those informal, free-flowing floorplans were pioneered by modernist architects like Boyd and Seidler. Domestic modernist architecture in Australia embraced natural light, industrial building materials and, most emphatically, the surrounding environment. Mid-century modern homes were built *into* the land, rather than plonked on top of it. A country that for so long was welded to frilly Victorian and Federation architecture, despite its blithe unsuitability to our environment, finally had a style of housing that acknowledged and embraced the landscape and conditions in which it was built.

The concept of open-plan, outward-looking architecture resonated strongly with Australians and their casual, outdoorsy lifestyles. Modernist homes were built for real life and acknowledged that we weren't living in late-19th century London. Prissy ornamental touches were forbidden. Instead, floor-to-ceiling windows allowed the sun to pour in and textured stone walls and timber panels brought warmth and character.

Today, a growing number of home buyers, depressed by the thoughtless design of contemporary housing, are looking again to mid-century modernist homes for inspiration and dedicated websites – and even real-estate agencies – have sprung up in response to the renewed interest in mid-century design. It's heartening to see this timeless, accessible and beautiful style of home finally gaining recognition for its role in changing the way Australians lived.

Sydney Mardi Gras

It's startling what a difference 40 years can make to the cultural climate of a country. In 1978, homosexual acts were still illegal everywhere except South Australia and the Australian Capital Territory. It was a dark and dehumanising spectre for anyone whose sexuality didn't fall within the traditional spectrum of what was understood to be 'normal'.

So in 1978, Sydney's LGBTQI community decided to make some noise about it. Intended to be Australia's contribution to International Gay Solidarity Day, on 24 June 1978 around 2000 people met in Oxford Street for a street festival to call for an end to discrimination against gay and lesbian people in housing, employment and the law. From those modest beginnings as a protest march sprang what is now one of the biggest gay pride events in the world, drawing an estimated crowd of 300,000 spectators each year. Mardi Gras features prominently in Sydney tourism campaigns and publishing behemoth Conde Nast named it 'one of the world's top ten dress-up parties' – a reputation well deserved. About 12,000 participants, variously decked out in angel's wings, drag, showgirl garb and a lot of bare flesh, take to the streets in an unhinged, life-affirming display of love, acceptance and glitter.

Sydney Mardi Gras

Every parade begins with 200 of the gloriously named Dykes on Bikes riding up Oxford Street accompanied by a show of fireworks. They're followed by floats representing everyone from the Australian Defence Force, ANZ bank, the Labor, Liberal and Greens parties (not on the same float, naturally) and the Department of Foreign Affairs, to Gay Tradies, Fitness Fairies and the Balloon Artists and Suppliers Association. Kylie, Cyndi Lauper, Jimmy Barnes and the late George Michael are among the many big-ticket celebrities who've performed at the post-parade party.

Despite the vocal protests of a few sections of the community – notably the fire-and-brimstone Reverend Fred Nile, who leads a prayer for rain every Mardi Gras day – the parade has been largely embraced by mainstream Australia. For all its OTT revelry, the underlying message remains a serious one: that no one should be bullied, harassed and denied their basic human rights because of their sexuality. The ever-increasing acceptance of LGBTQI rights by a significant majority of Australians shows that it's a message that's finally getting through.

Sydney Olympics

Were the Sydney 2000 Olympics 'the best Olympic Games ever'? Juan Antonio Samaranch, the then-president of the International Olympic Committee in 2000, believed so, making that bold proclamation during the closing ceremony of the Games. For a $2.2 billion taxpayer contribution, you'd be hoping for a pretty good outcome. Luckily, most of Australia felt the same way as Samaranch and an attitude of pride and glee permeated the streets of the entire country, as we watched the world watching us – and who doesn't enjoy an audience of billions?

The opening ceremony on 15 September set the tone for the two weeks that followed. A shamelessly OTT spectacle of Australiana, the show saw 13-year-old Nikki Webster and a cast of 12,687 performers take the audience on a four-hour journey of our history, icons and landscape. A Ken Done banner emblazoned with our famously laconic greeting, 'G'day', welcomed the global television audience of 3.7 billion to Australia. Driza-Bone clad stockmen on horseback, 120 of them, galloped across the stadium during a tribute to Banjo Patterson. There was corrugated iron. There were sheepdogs, beaches and bushfires. There was everything but John Farnham and Olivia Newton-John. Oh, wait – they were there, too!

Sydney Olympics

The ceremony may have mined every cliche in the country, but it was executed with such heart and verve that few could muster sufficient bile to get snooty about it. Despite a hair-raising glitch with the Olympic Cauldron – which, after being lit by Cathy Freeman, hung suspended in mid-air for an agonising four minutes before finally making its way to the roof of the stadium – the ceremony was an unqualified triumph. 'Wow! A colourful and colossal kaleidoscope on overdrive. Fan bloody 'tastic!' wrote Peter Fitzsimons in his appraisal of the opening ceremony for the *Sydney Morning Herald*.

It was never going to be an easy job outdoing the spectacle of a cherubic 13-year-old flying across the Olympic Stadium. But fortunately, our swimmers managed to, winning 18 medals. Ian Thorpe won three gold and two silver medals, surpassing the achievements of every other athlete in the games. He also earned a world record in the 400-metre freestyle. Grant Hackett took home gold, Susie O'Neill silver, Kieran Perkins silver, and Liesel Jones, the youngest medal winner at 15, silver. On the track, Cathy Freeman had a stunning gold medal victory in the women's 400-metre race.

There was legendary stuff brewing in the bars of Sydney, too. At Darling Harbour's Slip Inn, a 28-year-old Taswegian sales executive hit it off with a bright-eyed, boyish Dane. He turned out not to be a horny backpacker, but a prince. In 2004, Crown Prince Frederick made a princess of Mary Donaldson, now better known by her official Australian title of 'Our Mary'. Fred and Mary have produced a gaggle of attractive children and appear, despite the hysterical yelps of tabloid magazines, very happy together – a literal fairytale Olympics story, to add to the many that were written in Sydney's spring of 2000.

SWEARING

Australia: Magic mirror on the wall, who's the foulest-mouthed of all?

Magic mirror: Over the seven-jewelled hills, beyond the seventh fall, dwells Australia's people, foulest-mouthed of all.

When Australians take a shine to something, they embrace it with an almost pathological degree of enthusiasm. Footy is often described as a religion and accordingly, is given more screen time than God.

And swearing. We do like swearing. We like it so much that when politicians are looking for a quick boost in the polls, they swear on telly. We like it so much that people moving to Australia for work are warned to expect more profanity in the workplace than they might be used to. 'It's not uncommon to hear Australian managers swearing in a meeting ... while cursing is considered inappropriate in many business settings, Australians are motivated by vibrant, humorous and border-line vulgar speech,' *Business Insider* helpfully advises white-collar arrivals new to our shores.

We like swearing so much that language experts have suggested our mouths are among the foulest in the world. And, like any addiction, our swearing habit transcends socio-economic status, race, even religion; even your (OK, my) devout Christian,

Swearing

all-round good-guy neighbour might well believe in the cathartic properties of a well-timed C-bomb. Former prime minister, Kevin Rudd (also a devout Christian), swore on primetime TV when he described an economic headache as a 'political s**t storm'. The Opposition promptly claimed Rudd's profanity was a carefully scripted blunder, designed to curry favour with 'workers'. Scripted or not, the Opposition's response to Rudd's swearing is in itself telling: only in Australia could a polly swearing on TV be accused of cynically attempting to endear himself to voters. No US President or British PM would dream of letting a blue word slip in public, much less *premeditatedly* swear on TV. Rudd had notable form in the swearing arena, though. In 2012, leaked raw footage of a satellite call to China showed him unleashing eight F-words in less than two minutes.

The rest of the world obviously isn't quite as laid back as we are when it comes to swearing, as Tourism Australia learned the hard way in 2006. Their infamous Lara Bingle-fronted ad campaign, 'Where the bloody hell are you?', created something of a, well, s**t storm. It was banned in the UK and Canada and pared down to the rather less challenging 'So where are you?' for Singaporean audiences – all because of a word not even considered a profanity by most Australians.

On a more positive note, some psychologists believe that swearing is a survival strategy that we have developed in place of the grunts and shouts we once used to frighten off enemies and wild animals – evidence, perhaps, that Australians are the most highly evolved specimens in the world.

QANTAS

The greatest product placement in the history of cinema came courtesy of the 1988 film *Rain Man*, starring Dustin Hoffman and Tom Cruise. Hoffman's autistic character is scared of flying, but he *will* fly Qantas. And only Qantas. 'Why?' his exasperated brother (Cruise) asks. Because 'Qantas never crashed', replies Hoffman.

Cha-ching!

QANTAS

In a world in which around 25 per cent of people are scared of flying, it was as good as branding the brain of every nervous flyer in the world with the message, 'Fly Qantas!'. And if the fact *Rain Man* won four Academy Awards and grossed $354 million worldwide wasn't enough to reassure Qantas that a lot of people got the message, that was also the scene the Academy chose to screen during the nominee announcements on the night of the awards. The reaction of Qantas' competitors was swift and hysterical – 15 airlines cut the crucial, four-minute scene from the film in their inflight entertainment. Without it, the rest of the film was almost nonsensical. It was a pointless over-reaction – the film helped Qantas crack the American market and establish its worldwide reputation as the 'safe' airline.

Shameless plugs in Hollywood blockbusters would have been far from the minds of Wilmot Hudson Fysh and Paul McGinniss, when they started the Queensland and Northern Territory Aerial Services in 1920 with two wobbly old warplanes. The airline initially operated taxi and joy flights, in addition to airmail services subsidised by the Australian Government. In 1928, the Flying Doctors made their inaugural flight in a Qantas plane and by 1947 the Australian Government had bought the company. The airline was privatised again in 1992, with then-prime minister Paul Keating announcing the sale at a press conference and describing it as 'a little bit of history'. Qantas is now ranked the world's tenth best airline, according to air travel research firm Skytrax.

Qantas' history is distinguished not just by its work in the sky, but also by its characteristically Australian penchant for a bit of piss-taking. Attempting to crack the US market in the 1960s, Qantas ran a series of eye-catching print ads bearing the slogan, 'I hate Qantas'. The star of the ads was a peeved koala, imploring Americans not to come to Australia as he liked his peace and quiet. Something of a precursor to the wise-cracking duck of Air New Zealand's recent ads, the koala was a hit with Americans, who promptly boarded planes to Australia to meet these fluffy, querulous critters and were crestfallen on landing to realise that koalas sleep for 18 hours a day and have no particular beef with Qantas.

CLAIMING NEW ZEALAND STUFF AS OUR OWN

Citizens of New Zealand, we salute you. Since time immemorial, you have watched, bemused, as Australia flagrantly claims your best and brightest as our own. In the name of peaceful ongoing relations, let's try and settle the score once and for all on the question that hangs over Crowded House, Russell Crowe and the humble pavlova.

Presenting ... The Definitive Guide to Stuff that is Australian and Stuff that is New Zealand...err:

1) Crowded House – Two founding members, Nick Seymour and the late Paul Hester, were Australian. But as Mark Twain once said, two Australian band members do not maketh an Australian band. What *does* give our claim on the 'House some legitimacy, however, are the Australian inspirations behind many of the band's most famous songs. 'Four Seasons in One Day' was inspired by Melbourne's fickle weather. Neil Finn himself has said Melbourne was the 'birthplace of Crowded House, and was always the town we chose to return to. It's forever deeply ingrained in our collective psyche and was the backdrop for many of our best musical moments.' It's worth noting that Finn probably said this while contemplating the long white clouds above his palatial Auckland digs. Still. You don't argue with the singer of the band.

Verdict – Australia: 1
New Zealand: 0

2) Russell Crowe – Rusty spent the first four years of his life in New Zealand, then moved to Australia. He moved back to New Zealand in his teens and returned in his 20s. His two attempts to gain Australian citizenship have been rejected, according to Rusty himself. He owns multiple properties in Australia, half of the South Sydney Rabbitohs

CLAIMING NEW ZEALAND STUFF AS OUR OWN

rugby league team and is the father of two sons with his Australian ex-wife, Danielle Spencer. He loves a flannel shirt, a beer and a bit of biffo. Rusty, if the Australian Government won't do it, I'll grant you citizenship. The paperwork is in the mail.

Australia: 2
New Zealand: 0

3) Pavlova – Australia and New Zealand have long slugged it out over who can rightfully claim the fluffy white pav as their own. Unlike Neil Finn, the humble pav cannot speak for itself so we are therefore reliant on historians with a special interest in cake to answer the question of ownership. Professor Helen Leach appeared to have settled the score in 2008, with *The Pavlova Story: A Slice of New Zealand's Culinary History*. (The title sort of gives away which side of the fence she sits on.) Leach claimed the first pav was created in a New Zealand kitchen in 1929. So the score temporarily looked like this:

Australia: 2
New Zealand: 1

However, in 2015, some upstart cake historians, Dr Andrew Paul Wood and Annabelle Utrecht, threw a spanner in the works, claiming to have spent two years exhaustively researching the origins of the pav. Their conclusion? The modern pavlova began life as a German torte, before emigrating to the US, where it eventually became the pav. Our revised score board makes for sobering reading:

Australia: 2
New Zealand: 0

Obviously, our New Zealand brothers and sisters have not fared too well in The Definitive Guide to Stuff that is Australian and Stuff that is New Zealand...err. But chin up, Kiwis. You'll always have long white clouds and jandals (which FYI are actually called thongs, and on second thought are ours, too).

AUSTRALIAN ATTIRE

UGG BOOTS

Australia has given international fashion many gifts (blue singlets, Stubbies shorts, Coogi jumpers) but perhaps none more perplexing than Ugg boots, the aptly named sheepskin foot warmer.

Although Ugg boots have been haunting the soles of Australian feet since the 1970s, it wasn't until the '90s that Uggs began their bewildering ascent to the top of the international fashion heap. Kate Moss, Jennifer Lopez, Sarah Jessica Parker, Drew Barrymore and Jennifer Aniston have all been photographed wearing them and, surprisingly, there is little evidence to suggest they were forced at gunpoint to do so.

Ugg boots

Look, I'm not going to sugar coat this: Ugg boots make you look like a sheep that hurt its back jumping a fence and was then injected with a large quantity of sedative by a sympathetic vet. One's gait becomes slouchy and unhurried in Ugg boots – probably because they were never intended as anything more than a boot to warm the feet of shivering surfers on the beach. Their inventor, Shane Stedman, originally named them 'Ugh' boots, as that was the most common reaction to them. That first batch was, if possible, even less glamorous than today's boot: the sheepskin lining often still had bits of meat and sinew attached, which meant if you got lost in the woods in your Uggs, eating them for dinner was not out of the question.

Thankfully, the quality, if not the aesthetic appeal, of the boots increased as sales steadily climbed. In 1983, ten years after the company's inception, Stedman sold the rights to the name to a US company, pocketing a modest sum and the right to three pairs of free boots per year, before kicking up his sheep-skinned heels.

So it's not Stedman who's responsible for Ugg's recent foray into the summer sandal market. Not content with making our feet look stupid in winter, executives at Ugg decided they needed to look horrible in summer, too. Have you ever thought, 'Geez, hot summer we're having this year. I sure could use a fleecy sandal.' No? Neither has anyone else! But that didn't deter Ugg, which ploughed on ahead with a woolly sandal, untroubled by good sense or taste. It is almost impossible to describe the eye-watering awfulness of the Ugg sandal. One bemused tweet (of which there were many) described it as 'the mullet of the shoe world'.

Ugg *have* done the world one favour with their sheepskin sandals though – they've created the world's first chastity shoe. Thank God! Those belts are *really* uncomfortable.

Gumnut jewellery and Coogi sweaters

Youth of Australia, gather round and listen. There was a time when your nan didn't wear tasteful separates from Country Road, baby-pink cashmere scarves and muted-gold pendants. That nice old lady who cooks the Christmas roast and slips you a little cash when she knows your parents won't cough up for an iPod touch? She has skeletons in her closet. Or more specifically, she has gumnut babies, parrots and very busy jumpers in her closet.

The 1980s were a peculiar time for fashion and Australia did more than its fair share to contribute to the madness. Our unique connection with the bush, which once existed only in our hearts and minds, began to spread to our ears and necks as we adorned ourselves with gumleaf necklaces, dangly parrot earrings and cloisonné koala clip-ons. Don't bother asking your nan if she wore this stuff; it's a bit like asking her if she's a witch. She'll deny everything. But wear it she most certainly did, especially if she was an art teacher.

Of a more unisex nature was the psychedelic-puddle-of-colours-rendered-wearable-knit, the Coogi jumper, which, while associated with the '80s, only became an international sensation during the '90s. To say the Coogi was a 'busy' style of jumper is a bit like saying the Pope is a 'well-known' Catholic. Every square inch of a Coogi jumper could induce an epileptic seizure, with its blinding cords of rainbow colours heaped upon rainbow colours, heaped upon more rainbow colours, heaped upon a background of … rainbow colours.

AUSTRALIAN ATTIRE

GUMNUT JEWELLERY AND COOGI SWEATERS

From humble beginnings in not-so-humble Toorak, Melbourne, Coogi became a worldwide juggernaut, partly due to the brand's huge popularity within the hip-hop community. It's been name-checked in songs by The Notorious B.I.G., Kanye West and Australia's own Hilltop Hoods. Snoop Dogg has also been photographed wearing one. It's impossible to speculate as to why the Coogi jumper gained so much traction in the hip-hop world, but it's possibly related to the consumption of 'purple drank', the codeine syrup also made famous by hip-hop artists and DJs. The hefty price-tag of a Coogi jumper – anywhere from $300 to $700 – also gave it an appealing suggestion of opulence.

As stomach-churning as some of our jumpers may have been in the '80s, the era also signalled the beginning of Australian designers drawing fashion inspiration from our own shores, rather than attempting to emulate the runways of Paris. Great Australian fashion innovators like Jenny Kee, Jenny Bannister and Linda Jackson, among others, took their cues from the Australian landscape and culture. Their designs still startle and delight today thanks to their unmistakably Australian influences. So, if your nan has any of their designs lurking in her wardrobe – *steal them.*

BLUE BONDS
SINGLET

Commes des Garçons it is not, but the blue Bonds singlet is about as close as Australia gets to a national uniform. To don a ratty blue singlet is, essentially, to brand your head with the word 'STRAYAN'. But how, why and when did we fall in love with the blue singlet?

AUSTRALIAN ATTIRE

Blue Bonds singlet

It all began at the end of the 19th century. Champion shearer Jackie Howe understandably found the sleeves of his shirt too restrictive – and if you've ever shorn a sheep, you'll know it's not a task you want to undertake in your Sunday best. Shearing was hellishly demanding back in Howe's day. Sheds were filthy and vermin-infested, and the shears they used were a rudimentary affair similar to garden shears. Workers usually had to shear 100 sheep just to earn £1 ($1.65).

Howe came up with a novel idea to make the work marginally less uncomfortable – he hacked the sleeves off his shirt. Pretty soon, his mum was custom-making singlets for Howe, who, incidentally, was breaking all manner of shearing records throughout the colonies. Other chaps in the shed soon caught onto the sleeveless trend and began hacking the sleeves off their own shirts. Bonds started manufacturing their 'Chesty Bonds' singlets in 1920 and soaring sales confirmed that Australian men were desperate to get their pecs out.

They are widely known not as 'blue singlets' but 'wifebeaters' – owing to the singlet's association with working-class men, who, fairly or otherwise, have historically been viewed as those most likely to commit domestic violence. But in recent years, feminist activists have implored Australians to rename them 'respecters'. Well-intentioned as the campaign may be, it faces an uphill battle. When Australians christen something with a smart-arse nickname, they rarely abandon it in favour of a more palatable alternative. But don't just take my word for it. Head up to the Deni Ute Muster and ask someone in a 'wifebeater' what they think. In 2015, a respectable 3959 people donned the famous blue singlet at Deni to set the world record for the most people wearing blue singlets. You shouldn't have much trouble finding someone with an opinion (and, a word of warning, it's not likely to be pro-respecter).

THONGS

Argh, it's so annoying how everyone associates Australia with bloody thongs! As if we're a nation of people who spend all our leisure time dagging around the backyard or at the beach in thongs, shorts and blue singlets.

Annoying but, well, kinda true. Sure, you won't see thongs in a boardroom (probably), but you will see them almost everywhere else. There's a reason Kylie Minogue was perched atop a giant replica of a thong rather than a sensible brogue at the Sydney 2000 Olympics closing ceremony. Thongs are our national shoe – if it's not too much of a stretch to call a bit of floppy rubber a shoe.

THONGS

Vexingly, Australia cannot actually lay claim to inventing our beloved 'official casual shoe', which is one of the many things wrong with the world. The first thongs were actually produced around 4000 BC in Egypt and were made out of papyrus leaves. Which makes the ancient Egyptians the original bogans.

As fond as Australians are of them, it's just as well we didn't invent thongs, or we could be shouldering the blame for the thousands of horrific thong injuries incurred worldwide each year. Yes, really. Thongs can damage your health. We wear them because of their supposed convenience, yet, according to the UK's National Health Service, around 200,000 people present with thong-related injuries a year, draining 40 million pounds from NHS coffers. These are alarming statistics for a country with approximately one day per year in which thongs are seasonally appropriate footwear. No thong injury stats are available in Australia, but unless we have a continually evolving bogan supergene that helps us avoid thong-related injuries, one would assume the numbers are much higher than in the UK. Ideally, then, thongs should be viewed as more of a stationary shoe.

But the convenience of the thong will always trump any safety issues, at least in Australia. Their all-round compatibility with the good life is too seductive to warrant chucking them out in favour of a less risky sandal, or, perish the thought, a reef shoe. Thongs allow for maximum airflow during stinking summer heat, are the best way to protect your feet from burning hot sand and lend themselves brilliantly to hungover ambles to the milk bar for smokes and hot chips. Thongs give their wearer a strange, but not unappealing, hip-swinging gait, probably caused by the strain of trying to keep the damn things on your feet. If thongs could talk, they would say, 'I'm not in a hurry, mate. Let's have another beer'. Well, OK, if you insist, but you'll have to change your shoes first; the sign above the bar says 'no thongs'.

STUBBIES SHORTS

Clothes are strange things. Throughout history we humans have sipped on many a cup of fashion Kool-Aid, prompting us to wear pants that make us look like we're wearing a soiled nappy, or jeans that necessitate a full Brazilian wax before wearing. Women are generally the most common fashion victims, dutifully following the edicts of sadistic *Vogue* editors as they steer us down the road to sartorial suicide.

But before you start feeling smug about the lack of harem pants in your wardrobe, dear men, let the annals of fashion history show that you too have, on occasion, drunk from the same deadly cup. And no, I'm not talking about your Bintang tank top or mullets (although feel free to lose those babies anytime). Today we're going to talk about a teeny tiny piece of material you once wore to cover your junk – Stubbies. Let the word just roll around in your mouth for a moment. *Stubbies*. It's not sexy. 'Stubbing' is a word that implies painful squashing. It's a word appropriately devoid of any feminine overtones.

'The little shorts for big jobs', proclaimed ads announcing the arrival of Stubbies on the scene, and what a big job they did on the dignity of Australian males. Unleashed onto a wildly receptive public by clothing manufacturer Edward Fletcher in 1972, for a solid decade one could scarcely leave the house without fear of encountering a moustachioed gent with his gear piled like badly stored Christmas baubles into these shortest-of-short, tightest-of-tight pants. For those not young enough to recall the '70s, think Kylie Minogue in her gold hot pants, then imagine your neighbour Bruce mowing the lawn in them. Edward Fletcher and Co. sold 750,000 pairs in the first year alone, their runaway success prompting the company to change its name to Stubbies.

STUBBIES SHORTS

Aided and abetted by his Stubbies, a man could, and did, commit a cornucopia of fashion crimes. He could wear them with knee-high socks and grey leather shoes with zips, a look favoured by my year 8 science teacher. He could wear them with a canary-yellow short-sleeved shirt and a scratchy polyester maroon vest – again, a look favoured by my year 8 science teacher. He could wear them a size too small and develop a penchant for hoiking his leg up on the table when checking your school work, a pose also favoured by my year 8 science teacher.

It would be no exaggeration to say that, thanks to Stubbies, my memories of year 8 science class are as vivid as those of giving birth, expelling a gallstone and jumping out of a plane. Given the fact that, in 1980 alone, three million pairs of Stubbies were sold, there must be countless other victims of PTSD (Post Traumatic Stubbies Disorder). To you, friends, I say this: hit the op-shops and buy up those old Stubbies. Do not let them fall into the hands of hipsters for a cheeky revival. *We may not survive a second attack!*

Akubra

Have you ever bought an expensive new hat, removed it from its box, admired its impeccable craftsmanship from every angle, then stomped all over it before flinging it into a puddle?

   If you work in the country and own an Akubra, the answer is probably, 'Yes'. A pristine hat unsullied by the elements won't do for mustering cattle 10 hours a day, hence this brutal initiation for new Akubras. Although cattle farmers may not appreciate the comparison, it's a bit like a ballerina breaking in pointe shoes. A stomped-on hat is softer and more comfortable to wear and, perhaps just as importantly, shows you're unconcerned with prissy stuff like keeping your hat looking nice. Fortunately, Akubras can withstand a bit of stomping. After all, the family-owned company who make them doesn't design them with an evening at the ballet in mind.

Akubra

Akubras are made from wild Australian rabbits, with Belgian, French and Ukrainian rabbits also in the mix. A single hat (turn the page now if you own a pet rabbit) uses approximately 14 rabbit skins. Sixty people are involved in the making of a single hat and the 19-stage manufacturing process hasn't changed in 100 years. It's the antithesis of the cheap, fast clothing so abundant in modern life.

The Akubra story began with English hatter Benjamin Dunkerley, who emigrated to Glenorchy, Tasmania, in 1874 and set up a hat-making business. In 1892, he patented a fur-cutting machine that removed the hair tip from rabbit fur and which was adopted worldwide. The name Akubra is believed to be derived from the Aboriginal word for head covering.

Akubras are historically associated with our defence forces, and 80 per cent of the company's business once came from Australian Defence Force contracts, with more than two million hats produced for service men and women since World War I. From the end of World War II until the late 1950s, Akubra was making between 700,000 and one million hats every year.

One of our most iconic symbols and inextricably linked to working life in Australia, the Akubra is proudly plonked atop the pates of visiting dignitaries, pop stars and royal visitors. But in the beginning, the Akubra served a simple, vital function: shielding workers from the notoriously brutal Australian sun. For Australians who work the land, it remains exactly that. But for many others of a certain age the Akubra is associated with one man: Ian 'Molly' Meldrum. There's just one problem with this – Molly wears a Stetson, not an Akubra. Molly, for shame! That sort of behaviour is simply *un-Austrayan*.

AUSTRALIA ON SCREEN

NEIGHBOURS

Just as a medical intern can't expect to walk into a hospital and start performing open-heart surgery, nor can a new actor expect to begin their career doing Shakespeare soliloquies for Kenneth Branagh. That's why we have *Neighbours*.

Some people mistakenly believe *Neighbours* to be a moderately entertaining soap opera, high on suds. It is actually more like an early childhood education centre for future megastars. Guy Pearce, Margot Robbie, Natalie Imbruglia, Kylie Minogue and Delta Goodrem all got their start on *Neighbours*.

NEIGHBOURS

So why is it such a star factory? And why has it endured so long? Much of its success can be attributed to the fact that *Neighbours* never gets too caught up in itself. No matter how ludicrous the storylines (Harold getting lost at sea, only to reappear as a conveniently amnesiac tuba player with the Salvos band, comes to mind), the viewer always has a sense that the cast and crew are having a giggle between takes. It's a quality not shared by other primetime soaps. *Neighbours* has also taken care never to stray from the bog-standard suburbs many of us live in. Most of us don't answer the doorbell to find our dead ex-wife on the doorstep, miraculously resurrected (as Toadfish 'Toadie' Rebecchi once did), but we do live in similar streets, similar houses, mix with similar people and go to similar schools.

If *Home and Away* is the Australia that foreigners think we live in, *Neighbours* is the Australia that we *actually* live in. Its daggy charm has helped it to become the longest running television series in Australian history and a staple of British television, drawing an audience of 19 million a day during its 1990 peak. In 1987, episode number 523 was seen by two million viewers in Australia and 19.6 million in the UK and is still regarded as one of the most memorable moments in soap-opera history. It was, of course, Scott and Charlene's wedding (which may as well have been called 'OMG-Kylie-and-Jason-are-getting–married-on-*Neighbours*-do-you-think-they-will-in-real-life-too?').

To watch every episode of *Neighbours* would take a full 147 days. Making that much soap is no joke – six episodes of the show are churned out per five-day filming cycle. This is impressive stuff, given that most people have trouble producing one episode of a television show over an entire lifespan. Its huge popularity with Brits has given life to a perennially popular cottage industry of *Neighbours* tourism, with trivia nights and bus tours to Ramsay Street (actually Pin Oak Court, in Melbourne's Vermont South).

Australians have a bit of a cultural cringe about it all but, while we may not always love *Neighbours*, with a little understanding, it's hard not to like it.

THE
LOGIES

Laughter! Action! Excitement!
Forget it. You're watching the Logies.

Taking the piss out of the Logies is Australia's third favourite sport, after AFL and NRL. It doesn't take a degree in cultural studies to see why.

There's that name, for starters. The Logies were named in honour of the man who helped invent television, John Logie Baird. Bewilderingly, the organisers of the event decided 'the Logies' had a nicer ring to it than 'the Bairds'. Imagine how different things might have been: 'Australian television's night of nights, the Bairds!' It's hard to imagine an awards night called 'the Bairds' being held in the Zodiac Room of a cruise liner named *Fairstar, the Fun Ship*, as the Logies were in 1967.

THE LOGIES

The Logies celebrate everything about local telly of which we are slightly embarrassed, yet very fond, like *Neighbours*, *Home and Away* and Daryl Somers. They are voted for by 'the people', primarily readers of the delightfully daggy *TV Week*, the Logies' main sponsor, but network publicists are rumoured to engage in mass-voting to tilt the numbers in favour of their stars. All this makes the Logies a confusingly slippery proposition; egalitarian on one hand, slightly shady on the other. Consequently, nobody ever knows quite how to react to them, least of all the attendees. Is it glamorous? Is it tacky? Is anyone at home actually watching? How much free grog can I sink before I have to front the cameras to present the top-rating breakfast show?

Hosting the Logies is widely regarded as a poisoned chalice. One-time host Wendy Harmer compared it to cutting her own arm off with a blunt chainsaw. Gretel Killeen said it *killed* the person she had been. Bert Newton hosted the awards a record 19 times, but says he wouldn't do it now, given the buckets of hot molten poo flung at hosts via the internet (isn't social media wonderful?). In recent years, the gig has been redeemed by comedian Dave Hughes, whose inherent affability allows him to deliver sharp material while keeping the room smiling.

For all its lumps and bumps, the Logies have produced some fine moments in Australian history: the first swear word ever heard on Australian TV was courtesy of drunk US actor Michael Cole at the 1973 Logies; 1950's Gold Logie was presented to Denise Drysdale by John Wayne, making for some delightfully incongruous onstage banter; and in 1999, host Andrew Denton thanked 'the traditional owners of this land – the Packers' at the Crown Palladium Ballroom, before perching himself on the lap of a bemused James Packer (owner of both Crown and Channel Nine, long-time broadcaster of the Logies).

Here's hoping the whole affair never gets too straitlaced or upmarket. After all, this isn't the Bairds we're talking about.

Play School

It's impossible to get through the first five years of parenthood without being driven to the edge of despair by children's TV. Every parent has that one show that makes them feel like their brain is being stabbed by screaming goblins; the fabric of their soul shredded by wild dogs. Having a kids' show that really upsets you is a parental rite of passage, like being vomited on, and cleaning poo off a slippery dip.

But *Play School* is never that show. *Play School* presenters speak in regular 'inside' voices, rather than the apocalyptic disco shrieks favoured by so many other kids' shows. Miraculously irritant-free, it's the ideal choice to play on repeat on those glorious days when you are too sick to move, but still have a pre-schooler to care for.

Play School emerged in July of 1966, based on the English show of the same name, which wrapped up in 1988 after a piddling 22 years on air. *Play School* AU is now the second longest-running children's TV show in the world, after the UK's *Blue Peter*. The famously comely Benita Collings holds the record for hosting the most episodes of *Play School*, 401 in total. Presenters are of a uniformly high calibre, among them Noni Hazelhurst, Deborah Mailman, Justine Clarke, Essie Davis, Rhys Muldoon, Georgie Parker and Eddie Perfect.

Unusually for children's television, *Play School* hosts don't give off the aura of bored twenty-somethings killing time on baby telly until they score a gig as Foxtel VJ. They are all professional actors who submit to a rigorous audition process; a gig on *Play School* is one of the Australian screen's most coveted. Using props like the arch, round, square and diamond windows (still an exciting guessing game when you're pushing 40, truly) the hosts examine things in the outside world, like grocery shopping, cooking, school

Play School

and different cultures based around a weekly theme. Props like the rocket, flower and train clocks introduce children to the basic concepts of telling the time and counting. Presenters speak directly to the child at home through the camera, and each episode is scripted by early childhood experts. There are no large bobbly heads perched atop miniature bodies, serial-killer smiles or worms with human faces on *Play School*.

Despite staying largely true to its original, 1966 formula, it never feels tired or dated. Children, by nature philistines who hate anything older than they are, will happily watch a 30-year-old episode of *Play School*, as enchanted by Noni Hazlehurst, John Hamblin and Benita Collings as their parents once were. Forget iPads, iPhones and iPod touches, if you're looking for a peaceful half hour in which to deal with all your disconnection notices and bathroom mould, and can't afford a nanny, nothing beats *Play School*.

A Country Practice

Americans of a certain vintage are able to recall with crystalline clarity what they were doing on the day of JFK's assassination. Australian TV watchers of the 1980s can similarly recall every detail of Molly's 1984 death on *A Country Practice*. For a generation of Australian children, it was their first indication that, sometimes, young people die, too.

The death of the much-loved character dissolved an entire nation of viewers into weeping wrecks; a second viewing 30-plus years later confirms the scene has lost none of its power with age. Molly is depicted lying on an outdoor seat bundled up in blankets as she watches her (onscreen and off) husband Brendan fly a kite with their daughter, Chloe, in the backyard. Molly is clearly not long for this earth. Her eyes begin to close, the screen begins to fade, Brendan runs toward her and lets out an anguished scream – '*Molly!!!!!*'. Fade to black.

If this page of the book feels a little wet, it's because the publishers have smeared it with a droplet of the tears I'm shedding as I write this. Molly's death remains the most significant soapie demise this country has ever seen, the force of its impact a consequence not only of our affection for the character (played by Anne Tenney) but

A Country Practice

also of the scene's sense of being anchored in real-life experience. It's a scene that, unlike most soap-opera deaths, you can imagine happening to you or someone you know.

A Country Practice (ACP) was much more than just a cause of PTSD for viewers who witnessed Molly's death, though. Running for 1058 episodes from 1981 to 1993, it was produced by Channel Seven in Sydney. Screening twice a week for one hour, the show centred around the bucolic country town of Wandin Valley and its residents. Most of the action took place in the town's hospital, medical practice, RSL, police station and vet clinic. Unusually for the times, *ACP* was a comedy-drama that addressed issues such as domestic violence, suicide, drug addiction, infertility, HIV/AIDS, environmental activism, Indigenous rights and terminal illness.

At its height, *ACP* reached a worldwide audience of six million, screening in France as *A Couer Ouvert* ('Heart to Heart') in Germany as *Das Buschkrankenhaus* ('The Bush Hospital') and in Italy as *Wandin Valley* ('Wandin Valley'). The fame had deleterious effects on Fatso, the show's famously voluptuous wombat, however. He was dismissed from duties after five years due to problems getting along with the rest of the cast. The original Fatso was played by 'George' but he had to be retired after contracting a marsupial viral disease. Into his custom-made wombat shoes stepped 'Garth', who saw the show through to the end of its run. Shannen Doherty would later claim that her infamous diva antics on the set of *Beverly Hills, 90210* were inspired by Fatso the wombat.

A Country Practice managed to be wholesome and earthy while steering clear of the saccharine or holier-than-thou. Its place in the pantheon of legendary Australian TV is well deserved, but I will never forgive them for Molly's death. *Molly!!!!*

Kath and Kim

If Jane Turner and Gina Riley had some meaty raw material to work with in 1994, when they created characters Kath Day-Knight and Kim Craig, 2017 offers an obscene array of vacuous fads, fitness inspo and hollow spirituality to gorge on. The influence of the Kardashians alone would provide enough laughs to sustain an entire season. Kim would be thrilled to share a first name and a bubble-butt with KK and there would be Kardashian perfume in her house, Kardashian shape wear in her wardrobe and a Kardashian app on her phone. There'd be a lot of *The Block* and *Dancing with the Stars*, there'd be plenty of handy lifehack apps (Kath) and not-very-active wear (Kim). There'd be pulled-pork sliders (Kel, Kath's husband and butcher extraordinaire) and a vigorous passion for the newly formed Women's Australian Football League (Sharon, Kim's sports-mad bestie). It says much about how excruciatingly well drawn these characters were that it's so easy to imagine *exactly* what their lives would look like now.

AUSTRALIA ON SCREEN

KATH AND KIM

Kath & Kim began as a skit on Jane Turner, Gina Riley and Magda Szubanski's mid-1990s sketch comedy show *Big Girl's Blouse*, before debuting as a full series on the ABC in 2002. By the end of its second season, it was the highest-rating comedy show in Australia, and in 2007 it made the move to Channel Seven. For a while, Kath and Kim were the most famous (fake) mother-daughter duo in Australia. 'It's noice, it's different, it's unusual' may have been their catchcry, but it was precisely because they were *not* different, or unusual, or particularly nice, that Australian viewers embraced them like family.

Dead-eyed, desultory and self-obsessed, Kim was the suburban princess who would 'effing *knife* you' if you accidentally smiled at her boyfriend. The Kims of the world have always wielded disproportionate power; their deficit of charm and grace makes them terrifying friends, much less enemies. Kim exists seemingly to inject as much cattiness and bitterness as possible into the lives of those closest to her. Meanwhile, her mother, Kath, the tizzy, eternally chipper dynamo, deftly incorporated just about every quirk and characteristic of the suburban Australian housewife, right down to her cropped white trousers and clacky mules. Their lives revolved around trips to the local shopping mall, weight loss, celebrity gossip and fantasy weddings. There was hardly a detail that wouldn't induce a wince of recognition; everyone has had a Kath, Kim, Sharon or Kel in their lives.

'I think it's nice if you can't understand it, it's more elegant', says Sharon in one of the earliest *Kath & Kim* sketches, after Kath reads aloud an invitation to Kim's wedding she's just written: 'Bevan and Julie, you are honoured to be requested for the pleasure of your attendance at the Holy conubials of Kim and Brett, and afterwards to witness the conjugals in the privacy of our home.'

That 30-second scene summed up *Kath & Kim* better than any other, parodying the endearing quirks of suburban Australia in microscopic detail. Noice work, ladies.

PRISONER

Orange is the New Black? That show is strictly for thumb-suckers. Australia was doing women's prison drama well before many of the fine-boned inmates of Litchfield Penitentiary were even born. This was no minimum-security lark, either. *Prisoner*, set in the maximum-security H-Block division of Wentworth detention centre, screened for 692 episodes between 1979 and 1986.

'If you think prison is hell for a man, imagine what it's like for a woman', the commercials for *Prisoner* grimly intoned, and they weren't kidding. The show focused on the pain of being separated from family, prison hierarchies, friendships, recidivism, prison riots, and Bea Smith beating the crap out of various inmates and wardens.

The show was remarkably dark for a hit TV show that, at its peak, screened two new hour-long episodes per week. Even by today's blood-soaked standards, *Prisoner* is wincingly graphic in its depiction of violence and terror. The early episodes featured stabbings, burning and a hanging. One of the show's most iconic scenes featured 'Queen' Bea burning the hand of convicted child murderer Lynn in the laundry room's steam press.

PRISONER

Unlike *Orange is the New Black*, there were no lipstick lesbians at Wentworth, just lesbians. Nobody looked like they would be pursuing a career as a high-fashion model once their sentence was up. They were victims of bad circumstances, bad men, bad families, and social and personal injustices. Sometimes they were just plain bad: crime family matriarchs and murderers. Startlingly frank and brutal by today's standards, in the early 1980s, it was positively radical.

'Queen' Bea Smith (Val Lehman), boozy old Lizzie Birdsworth (Sheila Florance) and daffy, child-like Doreen Anderson (Colette Mann) were the axis around which the show spun. None had had an easy time of life; Bea was in prison for murdering her husband and his mistress, and her grief at the death of her daughter from a heroin overdose manifested in an incandescent loathing of drug peddlers. Doreen was a petty criminal who'd been in and out of juvenile institutions before landing in Wentworth. The chain-smoking alcoholic Lizzie had been in prison for 20 years at the show's outset, imprisoned for poisoning a group of shearers who complained about her food when she was a bush cook. It later transpired that someone else had in fact added the fatal dose of poison to the food; Lizzie had only put in enough to make them sick.

The show's ratings began to slide in the mid-'80s as glossier competitors vied for our attention. You can't keep a good show about bad girls down, though, and in 2013 *Prisoner* was reborn on Foxtel as *Wentworth*, which has gained a worldwide audience and international acclaim. Fortunately, this time around the producers have wisely avoided renaming the show for Canadian audiences, as they did with *Prisoner*. It's likely Canadian males were a little let down when they discovered that *Caged Women* was not about dancing girls in clubs, but gnarled female prisoners and malevolent guards delivering savage one liners like, 'have you ever thought of lacing up your mouth and renting out your head as a football?'

THE WIGGLES

Ready, steady, wiggle!
Emma, Lachy, Simon, and Anthony too!

Ready, steady, wiggle!

You can jump
like a kangaroo!

Ready, steady, wiggle!
Dorothy, Wags,
and Henry too!

Ready, steady, wiggle!
and Captain Feathersword,
woo-hoo!

Wiggle, wiggle, wiggle, wiggle, wiggle, wiggle,
wiggle, wiggle, wiggle, wiggle, wiggle, wiggle, WOO!

If you are the parent of a small child, right now you'll be shouting at this page in anguish, wondering why you can't do something as apparently innocent as *pick up a book* without being pummelled by yet another Wiggles earworm. Wiggles songs are like an STD. You cannot un-catch them.

There are no Wiggles Earworm Support Groups that I know of, but there bloody well should be – a detox clinic for parents who blithely ignored the 'CAUTION: Do not use for more than three days in a row without consulting a doctor' sticker on the packaging, and now hear Wiggles songs *even when no Wiggles song is playing*.

The Wiggles have done much to bring joy into the lives of children who would otherwise have only, um, other kids' shows for entertainment. The Wiggles are not stupid, tacky, or mean, and everything they do is imbued with a spirit of positivity. But that's not why parents buy the DVDs. They buy the DVDs because the Wiggles are

The Wiggles

catnip for children. When children are watching *The Wiggles*, parents have time for life's little luxuries, like going to the toilet alone and making spag bol.

The Wiggles were formed in 1991 by five Australian teaching students who had a hunch that parents of toddlers weren't being sufficiently tormented by the children's entertainment then on offer. Anthony Field and Jeff Fatt were originally in a band named the Cockroaches. A bit of a line-up change (Greg Page, Murray Cook and Phillip Wilcher were the only non-Cockroaches in the Wiggles' first incarnation). A change in number (down to four after Phillip Wilcher left the band). A change in lyrical direction – 'The Cockroaches sing about girls and love ... The Wiggles sing about hot potatoes and cold spaghetti', Anthony Field once said – and the addition of some colourful skivvies, and boom: worldwide sales of 23 million DVDs and seven million CDs. Since 2004, the Wiggles have regularly been listed as Australia's highest-paid entertainers. That's a lot of big red cars in the garage.

Various line-up changes for the band – Field is now the only remaining original member   have done nought to dampen children's enthusiasm for the boppy, accessible style of the Wiggles, and the introduction in 2013 of the band's first female member, Emma Watkins, proved a canny move. Watkins now has her own spin-off show, replete with characteristic earworm theme tune:

She's the girl with the bow in her hair
Everybody swing your hands in the air!
And sing E-M-M-A
Emma!
E-M-M-A
EMMA!

If the Australian Government ever begins to fret about the number of Australian citizens who don't know the words to their own anthem, they would do well to commission the Wiggles to do a rewrite. At least no one would ever, ever forget *those* words.

NUMBER 96

Dear Australian commercial television executives,

It's me, the ghost of the golden era of Australian telly. I've been watching you for a while now and I feel it's time we have a little chat about what telly can be when you don't make programming decisions based around ultra-conservative notions of what Australian people can cope with seeing on their screens. A little chat about how, for a country as diverse as Australia, our screens look very same-same.

Oh, and we're also going to have a little chat about *Celebrity Splash*.

Telly exec people, most of you are too young to remember *Number 96*, but I'm not; I'm a ghost. *Number 96* ran from 1972 to 1977 and pioneered the half-hour, five-episodes-a-week format now used by *Neighbours*, *Home and Away* and almost every other soapie in the world. On the day of its premiere, the network promos teased viewers with the line: 'Tonight Australian television loses its virginity.'

Commissioned by the fledgling Channel Ten, then known as Channel 0-10, *Number 96* was set in a fictional apartment block at number 96 Lindsay Street, Paddington. It was intended to be a racier version of the monster UK soap, *Coronation Street*. The end product featured an ethnically diverse cast of young, old, gay, straight, transgender and Aboriginal characters. There were boobs and bums and pantyhose murderers and bomb blasts, too, so it was hardly a solumn PC affair. The world's first gay TV character debuted on *Number 96*; not a campy caricature but a masculine, intelligent, level-headed lawyer in a relationship with a bisexual man. It was not just ground-breaking for Australian TV – nothing of its kind had ever screened anywhere in the world.

Number 96

And, oh, was it popular! Telly people, you can't imagine! There were spin-off cookbooks, cast LPs, serialised novels and even a feature film that smashed the box office. To be a star of *Number 96* was to attain Beatles-like fame and adoration. The cast travelled from Sydney to Melbourne for the Logies in a custom train carriage, *The Spirit of 96*, stopping regularly for a smoke and a meet-and-greet with fans, who swarmed the platforms at every station stop. They required a police escort on arrival at Flinders Street Station, such were the crowd numbers, and were mobbed at the Moomba festival. Australians not only accepted diversity on their screens, they went positively bananas for it.

The show didn't just have a diverse cast, either; it also tackled a raft of social issues. Heroin addiction, racism, alcoholism, breast cancer, rape – *Number 96* touched on them all and managed to throw a lot of bonking into the mix, too. It ran for 1218 episodes and in the years that followed its conclusion, network TV continued to push boundaries, encourage a diversity of ages and ethnicities on screen and explore difficult subject terrain.

Just kidding! You lot took over, and gave us *Celebrity Splash*, *Dancing on Ice*, and *The Bachelor*. But it's time to rethink your programming, which as it stands is equivalent to a cat dropping a headless rat on its owner's doorstep and expecting praise in return. Let's get bold. Let's get real. Let's get a lot more wobbly bits on prime-time television. And let's acknowledge it's 2018, not 1818.

It's time, telly.

Yours,

The ghost of the golden era of television.

Australian films

'Miranda! MIRANDA, DON'T GO!'

'That's not a knife – this is a knife.'

'I am the Nightrider. I'm a fuel-injected suicide machine. I am the rocker, I am the roller, I am the out-of-controller!'

'Tell him he's dreaming.'

'You're terrible, Muriel.'

Australian films have a habit of producing classic one-liners that quickly find their way into the national lexicon. Who could forget the blood-curdling screams of Edith imploring Miranda to stay by her side in *Picnic at Hanging Rock*? Or Mick Dundee's droll retort to a would-be mugger in *Crocodile Dundee*; the Nightrider's crazed rant after escaping police custody in *Mad Max*; Darryl Kerrigan scoffing at the asking price of second-hand ads in the *Trading Post* in *The Castle*; or Muriel Hemingway being taunted by her slovenly sister in *Muriel's Wedding*?

If none of that makes sense to you, it's time to bone up on your Australian cinema history. For a sparsely populated country, Australia has managed to produce a disproportionately high number of memorably excellent, bonkers, chilling, and just plain devastating films. We've also gifted the world with some of the sparkliest stars of the big screen: Errol Flynn, Cate Blanchett, Geoffrey Rush, Naomi Watts, Heath Ledger, Toni Collette, Hugh Jackman, Nicole Kidman, Ben Mendelsohn, Hugo Weaving, Mel Gibson and Rachel Griffiths.

Australian films

While in the years 1984-2016, just nine per cent of the films screened in Australia were our own, the homegrown movies that do manage to make it onto the big screen tend to leave quite an imprint. You don't need to have been of cinema-going age in 1975 to be familiar with the most famous line in Peter Weir's brilliantly unsettling *Picnic at Hanging Rock* – at some point or another, you've probably jestingly shouted 'MIRANDA! DON'T GO MIRANDA!' to a friend (and if you went to a girls-only school, you probably yelled it on an almost daily basis). Similarly, 'You're terrible, Muriel' can still be heard bouncing off the walls of lounge rooms and offices more than two decades after *Muriel's Wedding* was released 1994. True aficionados of the film will also jump on any opportunity to let rip with, 'I'M MARRIED! I'M BEWDIFUL!', parroting the words of bogan high priestess, Tania Degano (Sophie Lee) in the film's triumphant final scene.

Why do these lines resonate so deeply? Sometimes it's because of their familiarity – we've all been tormented by a Tania Degano. And sometimes it's simply because they're so eerie and the only way to deal with them is by turning them into a gag – never watch *Picnic at Hanging Rock* prior to going hiking. Or to bed. Or anywhere, really, other than in a well-lit environment with a support person.

Australians were early to catch on to the charms of the cinema and a well-established, if up-and-down, industry has existed since 1906. While it remains difficult for Australian films to command the audience numbers of American releases, a few Australian efforts still manage to break out each year. In recent years, Australian productions including *Red Dog, Mad Max: Fury Road* and *Lion* have stormed the box office and picked up a slew of international awards – all of which, you can bet, went straight to the pool room.

Published in 2017 by Hardie Grant Travel, a
division of Hardie Grant Publishing

Hardie Grant Travel (Melbourne)
Building 1, 658 Church Street
Richmond, Victoria 3121

Hardie Grant Travel (Sydney)
Level 7, 45 Jones Street
Ultimo, NSW 2007

hardiegranttravel.com

Explore Australia is an imprint of
Hardie Grant Travel

A Cataloguing-in-Publication entry is available
from the catalogue of the National Library of
Australia at www.nla.gov.au

100 Aussie Things We Know and Love
ISBN 9781741175493

Commissioning editor
Melissa Kayser
Project editor
Megan Cuthbert
Editor
Michael Ryan
Proofreader
Nick Tapp
Design
Vaughan Mossop
Typesetting
Michael Kuszla
Prepress
Michael Kuszla, Splitting Image Colour Studio

Printed in China by 1010 Printing International
Limited